I SAW
HIM
IN Y*O*UR EYES

OTHER BOOKS BY ACE COLLINS

Turn Your Radio On: The Stories Behind Gospel Music's All-Time Greatest Songs

Stories Behind the Best-Loved Songs of Christmas

Stories Behind the Great Traditions of Christmas

Stories Behind the Hymns That Inspire America

I SAW HIM IN Y*O*UR EYES

EVERYDAY PEOPLE MAKING EXTRAORDINARY IMPACT

IN THE LIVES OF KAREN KINGSBURY, TERRI BLACKSTOCK, BOBBY BOWDEN, CHARLIE DANIELS, S. TRUETT CATHY, AND MORE

ACE COLLINS

GRAND RAPIDS, MICHIGAN 49530 USA

ZONDERVAN.COM/
AUTHORTRACKER

ZONDERVAN™

I Saw Him in Your Eyes
Copyright © 2006 by Andrew Collins

Requests for information should be addressed to:

Zondervan, *Grand Rapids, Michigan 49530*

Library of Congress Cataloging-in-Publication Data

Collins, Ace
    I saw Him in your eyes: everyday people making extraordinary impact
in the lives of Karen Kingsbury, Terri Blackstock, Bobby Bowden, Charlie
Daniels, S. Truett Cathy, and more / Ace Collins.
        p. cm.
    Includes bibliographical references.
    ISBN-10: 0-310-26318-2
    ISBN-13: 978-0-310-226318-0
    1. Christian biography—United States. 2. Celebrities—Religious
life—United States. I. Title.
BR1700.3.C65 2006
277.3'082'.0922—dc22
{B}   2005019453

Interior design by Michelle Espinoza

Printed in the United States of America

---

06 07 08 09 10 11 • 16 15 14 13 12 11 10 9 8 7 6 5 4 3 2 1

For my parents,
whose sacrifice, faith, and giving
have been at the heart of everything they do

Contents

Introduction

What person had the most profound impact on your faith?

Who was the person in your life whose actions and words best reflected the Lord?

In whose eyes did you first see Jesus?

They say the eyes are a window to the soul. Over the past fifteen years I have had the opportunity to interview a number of people and ask them, "In whose eyes did you first see Jesus?" The stories they have told me have been fascinating and inspiring. These stories have given me glimpses into the foundation of the faith of people who have changed my life. I hope and pray their stories will impact you as well.

The heroes found in these pages are some of the greatest voices in the Christian world. When you get to know these heroes of the faith, you will discover that they reflect what they saw and learned from others who mirrored Jesus. Thus, while each chapter is a single individual's testimony, each chapter is also the story of the witness who was behind that hero's call to faith.

In these pages you will find the story of a Sunday school teacher who reached out to a quadriplegic, and, in the process, changed the whole world. You'll see the impact of grandfathers, grandmothers, aunts, mothers, and fathers on the lives of young children who would later become well-known singers, business-people, and writers. And you'll see how even the prayers of little-known neighbors and strangers made a profound difference in one woman's life.

Thanks to Zondervan, I was able bring these special stories to life. Now you can read about the faithful everyday believers who inspired some of the world's best-known and most-influential Christian voices. You can see how a simple touch, a look, or a word dramatically changed the world. You can even come to realize that if you put your faith into action, others will see it and want to embrace that faith as well.

I think these stories will inspire and move you. I believe you will enjoy this book and come to a greater understanding of the heroes profiled here. Yet I hope that something else also happens as you read *I Saw Him in Your Eyes*. I pray that you will remember the person in whose eyes you first saw Jesus. Then I pray that the next person who looks into your face will say, "I saw Him in your eyes."

1

The Power of Unknown Prayers

Nancy Coen

Founder of Servant Ministries

Nancy Coen is a wife, a mother of three, and a grandmother, yet she has the energy of a college student and the enthusiasm of a three-year-old child. First appearances would lead most to believe she is a successful businessperson. She once was, but this dynamo is now the founder and leader of Servant Ministries, an organization whose main thrust is taking the gospel into areas where believers are persecuted and even killed. Traveling 380,000 miles a year, the diminutive woman with the big smile and booming voice constantly puts her life on the line in the most dangerous places on the globe. She really lives the Great Commission each day of her life.

Nancy's story is a testament to the power of prayer. It is a dramatic narrative of stubborn resistance and faithful obedience. This story shines a bright spotlight on the dedication of those who simply will not give up on people.

"As a young child I saw a lot of things that bothered me about the Christian faith," Nancy recalled. "I was raised in a very legalistic church. As soon as I got away from home, I turned away from the church and vehemently turned against all things that I considered Christian. I would have sooner spit in the eye of a Christian than talk to them. At that time I even actively campaigned against Christian programs and missions."

As a young wife, mother, and businesswoman, Nancy wanted no part of God. Living in Indiana, she was a member of the local social set, a country-club regular, a loud boisterous woman who loved a party and embraced a "live for the moment" lifestyle. Though friendly and likable, she was a voice against any type of religion worming its way into her life. She didn't want to hear a prayer before a high school football game or have a local Christian youth group meet in the school. She taught her children there was no higher power and that Christianity was a fable.

"One day my daughter ran across the rural road where we lived to retrieve a ball that had landed in the yard of some folks who had just moved into our neighborhood. These were anything but my kind of people. They were poor and uneducated. They had no social skills. I didn't even like having them on the same street where I lived.

"When my daughter got into the yard, she was invited into their home. At that point I marched across the road to go get her. When the husband opened their front door, this Jesus music started coming out. And I thought, *These people are not only ignorant and poverty-stricken but on top of everything else they are Christians!*

"I was so upset that I would not let my daughter go back to their house again."

But the man who greeted Nancy at the door had not been put off by his neighbor's lack of respect for his family or his faith. In fact, he felt a call from God to pray for Nancy. Beginning that day, and continuing for seven years, he and his family prayed that Nancy would give her life to Jesus. They even involved their church in this practice, telling friends that this atheist would someday be used by the Lord to affect the lives of people all over the world. Anyone who knew Nancy would have scoffed at the idea of this ever happening.

"The interesting thing about this situation," Nancy remembers, "is that I never spoke to that man again. Three months later we left Indiana and moved to Texas. Yet I later found out through friends that he and his wife took seriously that call from God, and every day for seven years they prayed for me to be saved."

Seven years later Nancy had not changed. She was still a hard-hearted militant nonbeliever who felt the only light in the world came from either the sun, the moon, or a bulb. Yet with a family and church still praying for her, the successful businesswoman was about to find herself in a situation that nearly scared her to death.

"One day I woke up and I began to hear voices. The first one said, 'Behold, I stand at the door and knock.' Then a second voice would cry out, 'You know Jesus is dead and in the grave and never coming back.' Then a third voice popped up saying, 'I loved you so much I gave my Son for you.'"

The voices continued to war in her head all night long. At the time she believed she was going crazy.

"My mother had mental problems. She heard voices. She would cry for days on end. I now thought I was going through the same thing. I was going to be crazy like my mother. I had three small children and three successful businesses. I didn't have time for this. Finally, after several nights of this, I actually shouted down the hallway, 'I don't believe in God, I won't pray, and You can't make me!' Even at that moment I realized how funny it sounded for me, an atheist, to be telling God to get away from me."

The voices tormented Nancy for an entire week. During this time she became a basket case, exhausted, frazzled, and completely out of control. On her eighth night of not being able to sleep, she finally gave up, deciding to get on her knees. Not knowing how to pray, she simply repeated the prayers she had learned in childhood. They did nothing to ease her mental anguish.

"My prayers were not getting beyond the walls," Nancy recalled. "I finally confessed, 'I don't know how to pray. If You want me to pray, You are going to have to tell me how to pray.' Even though it was night and very dark, I saw a bright light right in front of me. I knew the Lord was there, and I was so scared I repented for everything I had ever done wrong in my whole life."

The next morning Nancy was a different person. The first thing she did was race to a local bookstore and buy a study Bible. For three days she constantly read the only Bible that she had ever allowed in her home. Overcome with passion to share her joy with others, she drove into the worst sections of South Texas towns and sought out prostitutes, drug addicts, alcoholics, and homeless people. She didn't just witness to them, she brought them back to her home, cleaned them up, fed them, and allowed them to sleep there. Needless to say, it took her family awhile to understand and adjust to the new Nancy.

At church and on her own, she tried to reach out to everyone she saw. Yet in time Nancy understood that this dynamic transformation must have taken place for a specific reason. Through prayer and study she came to realize she had been called to take her strength and conviction into regions of the world where Christians were persecuted. Selling her businesses, she founded Servant Ministries and began to travel to every corner of the world, not just telling her story to the lost but finding ways to meet the needs of the poorest and most mistreated Christians on the globe.

Over the course of the next decade, in the Middle East, Asia, Africa, and South America, Nancy was confronted by radicals from every one of the world's major religions, and a few she had never heard of. She was locked in jails and had her life threatened more times than she could count. Buoyed by the knowledge that many of those who had persecuted her had later accepted the Lord, she fought on. Yet even seeing miracles, conversions, and great movings of the Holy Spirit did not prepare her for what she was to witness in 1993 in Red China.

"I knew it was a divine appointment that I should meet the man they called 'The Greatest Living Martyr of China,'" Nancy explained. "We communicated before I left, and I told him I was going to bring Bibles to his church. On the day I was supposed to meet with him, we were arrested and we got caught with the Bibles. Because we were Americans we got only a little wrist slap, but they took our Bibles and assigned armed guards to follow us wherever we went in China. When I got back to my hotel, in my mailbox was this little rice paper. Written on the paper was, 'Dear Mrs. Coen, the whole church is waiting for you to arrive with the Bibles.' Of course I knew I was not going to be able to do that. If I had been caught even going to his house now, he would be arrested.

"Traveling with us was a native Chinese man who had been riding in a different train car when we were arrested. He had tossed his bags of Bibles out the window. He went back and got them later. That night a strategy came to me to take those three bags four blocks down and put them in storage at another hotel." Like a spy on a mission, she moved the books in the dead of night.

Nancy would spend ten more days touring China, but with the government guards always watching, she had no opportunity to deliver the Bibles. On the group's final night in this ancient nation, they decided to tour a slum in Shanghai. That is where they lost their tails. With no one following, Nancy hurried back to retrieve the stored Bibles. She grabbed two of the seventy-pound backpacks and flagged down a rickshaw driver. She gave him the address and climbed in.

"It took two and a half hours to find the man's house," she recalled. "The bottom floor of this house was a police observatory. They were monitoring this man. On the police office door was a sign written in seven languages, 'It is against the law in the People's Republic of China for anyone to enter these premises for the purpose of worshiping Jesus Christ.'"

Nancy was fortunate; no one was at the office at the time. More than a little scared, she opened a small door leading to the place assigned for her meeting and was faced with a narrow stairway that seemed to go on forever. Dragging the heavy back-packs behind her, she began her long, difficult climb.

"I got up to the second floor, but no one was there. I began to pray, but no one came. I was here to deliver these Bibles. This is why I came. This was my assignment. I began to cry because I was going to have to leave China and never know if these books got into the hands of the people to whom they were intended.

"I was sitting sobbing and noticed a ladder leading up to the attic. So I climbed it. There was nothing in the room but tree stumps nailed to the floor with two-by-eights lying across them. I now knew this was the place I was supposed to be."

Nancy waited for more than three hours on one of those homemade pews, but no one came. Realizing she had to get back to the hotel to prepare to leave China, she stood up. Then she heard what sounded like a broomstick hitting the floor. A wave of fear rushed down her spine as she turned toward the noise. And then she noticed a false wall leading to a hallway.

"I didn't know what to expect. Out from behind the wall came a little old lady. Her eyes had been burned out with hot pokers and her ears cut off because she had dared to share the gospel. She looked at least one hundred years old and couldn't have weighed eighty pounds.

"She appeared to be listening, through that hole where her ear had once been, as if she might have thought I had left."

"Hello," Nancy called out.

The woman, overcome with emotion, cried out, "American, American," and started jumping up and down. Suddenly the room's shutters pulled back and children poured in from off the roof.

"I looked around and was surrounded by kids whose parents had been taken the night before in a raid on the church. When they heard me coming up the stairways with my heavy book bags, they thought I was the police. They had been waiting for me to leave. Now they came in and were singing and dancing. It was such an awesome, beautiful moment. Then the woman grabbed my hand and pulled me away from the children and behind this false wall."

Nancy now found herself in a narrow hallway barely two feet wide. At the end of the hall was a bookshelf. On that shelf were eighty-nine copies of the New Testament. Nancy would discover that each had been hand copied by one of the church's children. They had added one page per day for years.

As Nancy studied one of the Bibles, the tiny woman put her shoulder to this bookcase and shoved it out of her way. There, in a five-and-a-half-feet-long by three-and-a-half-feet-high room, lying flat on his face on the floor, was the man she had come to meet. He was praying.

"He had been in that room for ten days praying that I would find a way to get this little church those Bibles," Nancy explained. "When he saw me he sat up and crawled out. Though there was little light in the hall, his face was so illuminated and bright it was almost blinding. After he told me he had been praying for my visit, I asked him what I could do for him to make his life easier. This beautiful smile came over his face as he said, 'The devil tempts the body of Christ in two ways: one is with intense persecution; the other is with abject apathy. I wouldn't trade one lash on my back, or any day of my twenty-eight years in a prison, for all the money in America. You have done what needs to be done for me already; you have prayed and you have come.'

"At that moment I looked straight into his eyes and knew that I was seeing God. My life has never been the same."

Nancy left China that night, but the man who is simply called "The Living Martyr of China" has never left her. Seeing Christ in this persecuted man's eyes pushes her daily with a new fervor to share the gospel with the lost. It is a journey full of dangerous peril, but as this former atheist puts it, "God is sending me to places I have never been, but He is also always there to meet me when I arrive." The journey from atheist to believer began with a short trip across a country road and has evolved into traveling around the world time and time again. And wherever she goes, Christ is at the heart of Nancy's vision.

2

Faith Knows No Limits

Elizabeth Swank & Ron Ballard

Sunday School Teacher and Christian Visionary

It was just another Saturday night for Elizabeth Swank. She was going over the last-minute details of a Sunday school lesson she would be teaching the older high school and young college students the next day at Sagamore Hills Baptist Church in Fort Worth, Texas. She had just completed her final notes when the phone rang. Knowing it was far too late for a normal call, she anxiously glanced over at her husband, Fred, the pastor of their church. After he answered, he listened for a moment, then closed his eyes and shook his head, saying, "We'll be there as soon as we can."

Looking over to his wife, Fred whispered, "It's Ron; he's been in a horrible accident."

In 1952, Ron Ballard was the prototypical all-American. Handsome, strong, clean-cut, and athletic, he was the poster boy of what heroes were supposed to look like. Yet for Ballard this was not just a skin-deep image. A leader in church and school, he was confident, smart, and levelheaded, seemingly destined for greatness. Yet in a brief instant on a long stretch of Texas blacktop, Ron's world would suddenly and dramatically change. This horrific transformation would ultimately not only redefine life for Ballard but—thanks to the support of his Sunday school teacher—change the lives of millions of others as well.

Ron had spent that Friday evening watching a friend play football in Stephenville. As he left the game, lightning flashed across the night sky. A front was moving in, cold air colliding with warm. As two stubborn forces of nature fought it out over the plains, heavy winds and rain pelted Ballard's windshield. His six-foot-five-inch, two-hundred-pound body tensed, fully ready to precisely react to any situation. As the storm intensified, the twenty-year-old eased his foot off the accelerator and dimmed his headlights in an effort to see down the dark highway.

Suddenly, between the slow sweeps of his wipers, Ron saw something move. Using the agility and reactions that had made him a star on the basketball court, he jammed the brakes to the floorboard and turned the wheel away from the shadowy image. Peering into the darkness, he saw nothing but blackness. For a split second he wondered if his eyes were playing tricks on him. Then, as a flash of lightning bathed the night in a bright yellow glow, he recognized what could have been a ghost from Texas history. In the midst of nature's fury a horse and rider were galloping down the middle of the highway!

Turn the wheel, his mind screamed at him. *Stop the car. Do something!*

There was simply no time to react. The auto caught the horse with the grill, bumper, and driver's side fender. Through the drone of millions of heavy raindrops, metal groaned as it bent and crumpled under the strain of the impact. The horse was flipped skyward, flying like an awkward Pegasus for an instant, then hurtling down through the darkness over the driver's seat. Ron watched in horror as the animal filled the windshield. He automatically closed his eyes and tried to scream, but his voice caught in his throat. Then he heard the windshield shatter and felt an incredible weight crushing his chest. A split second later there was nothing but blackness.

"Got to push my way out," he whispered. Yet as he mentally moved to his right and dropped his hands off the wheel, nothing happened. *What's going on? Why can't I feel my feet?*

As water rolled down his cheeks, Ballard thought, *I must be dying.* Strangely, that didn't scare him. He confronted the fact as easily as he did a tough zone defense. He was ready to meet the Lord. He had been for years. In Mrs. Swank's Sunday school classes, he had learned that as good as things were here, it was better on the other side of life's river. Yet death did not come to greet him on this night.

Within forty-five minutes, as Saturday, November 22, 1952, became Sunday, an ambulance arrived and rushed Ron Ballard to Harris Hospital in Fort Worth. Hours later, doctors determined Ron had broken his neck and would probably never move again. They informed Ballard's parents it would be miracle if he lived through the day. It was time to say goodbye.

First Ron's parents, then Fred and Elizabeth Swank, went to the young man's bed. They prayed for him, told him how much they loved him, and through tear-streaked eyes, they said goodbye. And even though all of them had the faith of Job, each wondered why this terrible tragedy had happened to their all-American.

A thousand images crowded into Elizabeth Swank's mind that long night. She thought of Ron as a gangly young teen, the nights she had seen him race across basketball courts, and the times he and a host of other youths had sat in her living room swapping stories and drinking soft drinks. She remembered some of his insights in Sunday school class, the manner in which his head tilted when he asked a question, and the way the girls always rushed into the room to try and get the seat beside him. He was remarkable in every way a boy could be. Now, to everyone who waited at the hospital, all the things that made Ron special seemed to have left his body and simply disappeared. And for the moment this strong Christian woman didn't even know how to pray. What could she ask for that would heal this situation? It would take a miracle, one greater than she had ever witnessed, for Ron just to live, much less ever do anything for himself or the world again. A few hours later, greeting Ron's friends as they walked into her Sunday school class, Elizabeth still had no answers. Yet she had the faith to tell her charges, "God will find a way to use this situation."

The strength Ron had used so gracefully on the basketball court kept him alive. Defying all expectations, he lived through not only the first night but the next and the next as well. Yet as the days turned to weeks and the weeks to months, while the all-American continued to breathe, he did little else. His strong muscles disappeared, and the body that had never failed him on the court would not respond to any command he issued. The all-American, "the boy most likely to succeed," the leader who had once set the course for all his peers, was for all practical purposes dead.

For the next eight months the hospital was Ron's home. He could talk, but he had run out of things to say. He could see, but the view never changed. He came to realize he was nothing more than a burden, dead weight in a world in which there was little compassion for those who could not fend for themselves.

For Elizabeth, Ron's life remained as vital as her own. She came to visit him several times a week and always on Sunday afternoon to tell him about what happened in Sunday school that morning. She also retaught the lesson just for him. And she always smiled, a smile that somehow brought assurance to Ron. In fact, Elizabeth's visits were about the only thing Ron looked forward to each week.

A year after the accident, Ron was told he would be sent home to live. Ironically, the news made Ron want to kill himself. For hours he tried to conceive of a way he could mercifully end his horrible life. Yet there was no route of escape, no way out. He was trapped. Then his condition fully hit him. He was doomed never to do anything for himself or anyone else again. His room would be his tomb.

In 1953 the world was not prepared to deal with the severely handicapped. Quadriplegics were simply sent home to lie in bed and wait for death. And that is what Ron did. Yet his heart would not quit beating; his lungs would not quit breathing. Ironically, it seemed that the only thing he was really good at was staying alive.

Though his parents remained devoted to him as they cared for his every need, Ron felt like a baby. He wanted to be more than that. He had to find a reason to live. Ultimately Elizabeth Swank would help him find that reason. For a time her visits sustained Ron from one week to the next. He lived for them. Before each visit he was awash in loneliness and self-pity, but this dear woman always gave him new hope. She not only took the time to come see him; she also talked to him as if he were a whole person. For a few minutes each week, he felt there was one person on this earth who still considered him a man. When he looked deeply into her eyes, he felt as if he were looking directly into the eyes of Jesus.

As his Sunday school teacher continued to buoy his spirits, the winning drive that had made Ron a great athlete began to resurface. While he knew he could not change the fact that he couldn't move his body, by drawing on his competitive nature, he found he could control his mind. One day, as he was lying in his room counting the holes in the ceiling tiles for the hundredth time, he shouted out loud, "I want to live!" Because of this change of attitude, he couldn't wait for Elizabeth's next visit so he could ask this wise woman, the only one who had not given up on him, "How do I begin to live again?"

As his one real connection with the outside world had come through his Sunday school teacher, Ron decided he wanted to go to church and again experience her class in person. He asked Elizabeth if she could arrange it. Each Sunday thereafter, two men came to his home and lifted him and his wheelchair into a car that transported him to services. To get to the sanctuary, he had to be dragged up more than twenty steps, and then his wheelchair was placed in the building's slanting aisle. Belts strapped to the pews kept him from falling onto the floor, but it was still uncomfortable, and his chair was often in the way of others as they walked down the aisle. Yet Elizabeth's smile assured Ron he was welcome, and that those who carried him up the steps and those who had to walk around him wanted him there. So, each week, he came back.

"I need to do something for others," he constantly told Elizabeth. She assured him that God would open a door for him to do just that. "Just keep praying, Ron, just keep looking! We will find it!" The strength of her voice convinced Ron that the teacher believed her words too.

As Ron continued to search for answers and direction, he began to wonder if there was anyone else like him in the world. He never saw another person in a wheelchair. No one ever talked about other people who had handicaps. Finally he asked Elizabeth if there was just one other person in the city who was trapped in a body that would not work. Who was battling to find a place where they didn't stand out? Who was looking for a world where they were not considered a freak?

The answer Ron received was both illuminating and frightening.

"Ron," she explained, "within a few miles of this spot there are scores of people who are either in wheelchairs or are blind or have any of a long list of other physical problems. Some were hurt in accidents like you. Others were injured in World War II or the Korean War. Some were born with their problems."

With a new mindset, an idea flashed across his mind. Ron realized he could have a mission; he could still serve people. He could still make a difference!

The next morning, Ron's mother called Elizabeth and held the phone for her son as he presented a radical idea for 1955. His voice at fever pitch, Ron announced, "You told me I'm not alone. You told me there are lots of folks like me right here in this city, and because of stairs and curbs and other barriers, there is no place they can easily go. So let's start a church for them. A place where folks like me can go. A place where we won't be pitied or considered freaks. A place not only to worship but contribute. A place where I can teach Sunday school and inspire folks like you have inspired me."

As the teacher listened, Ron excitedly described his vision of a building with a flat floor, ground-level access, and room for wheelchairs. A place where the handicapped could show one another love and support. Elizabeth then shared Ron's vision with her husband, and the preacher immediately understood that Ron wanted to create more than a building; he wanted to build a totally new concept. The pastor also realized this church could be free not only from physical barriers to the handicapped but also from the spiritual barriers that had been created by a negative self-image.

On January 8, 1956, the Crusader's Chapel, America's first barrier-free church, opened its doors. That morning ten people worshiped together. The chapel immediately became a place where people could go for divine and human inspiration. This church also became a building where the nondisabled people of the world could come and see the little things that the handicapped needed to function. For the first time the idea of tearing down barriers to the handicapped, such as steps and curbs, was spotlighted, initially in Ron's imagination and then in that building. This spotlight began to influence the way local builders and city engineers thought. Soon, thanks to lobbying by Ron and Elizabeth Swank's Sunday school classes, curb cuts became a part of downtown Fort Worth, and ramps led up to the doors of many public buildings. The movement that had its roots in Fort Worth spread to Baltimore and then nationwide. By the

1970s, there were scores of buildings the handicapped could easily enter.

Ron Ballard was sent home to die, but instead, thanks in large part to the faith of a Sunday school teacher and the lessons she taught him, he decided to find a way to help others live. Ron became a successful businessman, a dynamic force in the city where he lived, and it all started with the faith of a Sunday school teacher. When Ron looked into Elizabeth Swank's eyes, he saw Jesus accepting him. When Elizabeth looked into Ron's eyes, she saw Jesus living in the least of these. Together they inspired each other, put their faith into action, and changed the world for millions.

3

A Father's Example

Pat Boone

Entertainer, Writer, Speaker

Pat Boone never planned to become one of the biggest recording stars of all time. When he was twelve years old he didn't lie awake at night dreaming about becoming the youngest host of a national television variety show. As he walked the corridors of his Nashville high school, thoughts of million-dollar Hollywood contracts didn't concern him at all. If he wanted to become a bestselling author or write the lyrics to one of the most monumental movie themes of all time, he didn't tell anyone. Rather, what the young Pat showed was a desire to be the best at everything he did. He knew that in order to do this he had to work hard and study. And the young man set about accomplishing his goals of excellence without ever compromising his lofty principles.

Pat Boone is one of the most remarkable men of his generation. In the world of music he is listed by *Billboard Magazine* as the seventh-biggest recording artist in history. Only Elvis Presley sold more records in the fifties. Throughout his career, Pat's songs have held the number one position on the charts for more than two hundred weeks. He has sold more than forty-five million records and has earned enough gold and platinum awards to begin his own Fort Knox.

His list of starring motion-picture roles is long and varied. From *State Fair* to *The Main Attraction*, his talents have sold millions of tickets and made the studios hundreds of millions of dollars. But even more impressive than the twenty-five times he was top-billed is the fact that he wrote the words to the *Exodus* theme, a song that has touched tens of millions of hearts around the world.

Pat is also one of the most successful authors of his day. His many books have sold into the millions and have been translated into a host of languages. He is one of the few inspirational authors to constantly be courted by secular publishers. Even today at age seventy he is still selling records, sharing his faith with hundreds of thousands each year, and speaking about moral issues on programs such as *Larry King Live.*

Finally, as if all of this were not enough, over the past forty-five years Pat has raised hundreds of millions of dollars for numerous charitable organizations. His energy, vigor, positive approach to life, and desire to do the Lord's will have made him a role model for several generations. Yet this legend was initially directed and influenced by one solitary man.

"I've met a lot of saintly people in my travels," Pat explained, "people like Corrie ten Boom, Brother Andrew, David Wilkerson, and so many others. And each of these people have had real influences on my life. But the first influence, and probably the greatest, was my dad."

Pat was born in Florida but grew up in Nashville, Tennessee, the son of hardworking, God-fearing Archie Boone. The elder Boone had taken a job with his uncle's construction business when Pat was just a baby. It had been a long time since America had seen good economic times, and in spite of Archie's college degree, the growing Boone family was barely making it.

Pat's family lived on ten acres of land in a very modest home and clung to an old beat-up company pickup truck as their only source of transportation. For Archie Boone, the days began early and ended late. He spent most of his time tired, worn down by long hours, going too hard and too fast to ever find enough time to sleep and recover from both the farm chores and his regular job. Yet this straight, honest man never grew too tired to pray before his meals, study his Bible each morning, and make sure he and his family attended church. Even exhaustion and illness didn't rattle his priorities.

"Daddy was trained to be an architect," Pat explained. "He was a graduate of the University of Florida. Mama and Daddy married in Florida, and then he came up to work for his uncle, Jack Boone, at Boone Contracting.

"We had ten acres of land, which was good because Daddy's participation in the Boone Contracting Company didn't really provide enough money for him to feed and clothe his rapidly growing family. By the time I was in grammar school there were two boys and two girls. We had cows which my brother and I were taught to milk, an acre of produce which we helped cultivate, and from time to time we had chickens, rabbits, pigs, and turkeys. For a long time, things at home were tough."

Besides the hard work and uncertain times, the memories that seemed to rest most clearly in Pat's mind were of his days spent at the Church of Christ in Donelson, Tennessee. "Because I had been going to church ever since I was born," Pat recalled, "it was so normal, so ordinary, so commonplace for me to be in church that I didn't think much about it."

Many children whose families take them to church every Sunday never receive the real message of why they are there. Because church is the only time they see any evidence of their family's Christian walk, these children naturally don't look at getting dressed up, sitting on a hard pew, and being forced to behave as anything more than a meaningless ritual. Pat Boone was not one of these children. By the time he was in grammar school, he began to realize that when his family left church and headed toward home, Christ wasn't left behind in the sanctuary. Rather, this man called Jesus was even more alive at home than He was at church. His presence was a part of everyday life.

"For some reason," Pat recalled, "every once in a while, I'd get up real early. As I came out of my room, I'd see Daddy in the kitchen. He would be sitting there by himself, eating cereal and a piece of toast and studying his Bible. I began to realize that this went on every day. Daddy would be up by six in the morning, studying and reading. He taught a Sunday school class at church, and he didn't take it lightly. He studied six days a week just so he could teach that half-hour class on Sunday.

"As I grew older, I was increasingly impressed by what he was doing. Daddy usually taught young adults. I don't remember why or how I ever wound up being in one of his classes, but when I ended up there I discovered he was really an excellent teacher. He was always so prepared, and he really drew things out of people. He gave them a chance to express themselves, to tell what they'd learned, to explain how they felt and what they believed. His classes were a time of growing and sharing.

"I was deeply impressed by what he put into these lessons because he was such a busy, hardworking man. That translated in my mind and heart that God's Word was more important than anything else in life."

In the Boone house, family prayer and Bible study were a part of each day. Yet in Pat's mind, it was his father's early-morning efforts to grow that made the deepest spiritual impression. For as long as Pat could remember, Archie Boone was respected as a biblical scholar in their church, a man who knew the Word as well as any teacher. But it was obvious to his son that he didn't think he knew enough to stop. He was determined to enlarge his understanding of God and His plan.

Due in no small part to his father's influence, young Pat began to study his own Bible. He read it through from Genesis to Revelation. He wanted to know more about salvation, he wanted to find out more about Jesus, and he wanted to understand just what the Lord was offering to do for him. His reading and prayer seemed to mature Pat beyond his years. It also created a pattern of study that wouldn't end when his busy schedule took him all over the world. Like his father, Pat was now on a course to grow in the knowledge of the Lord.

"Through my study and what I had learned at home and church," Pat explained, "I realized that accepting Christ as my Savior was the most important decision of my whole existence. Of course Daddy taught me that, but I wanted to read and know it myself. When I was thirteen I walked down the aisle of the David Lipscomb Church of Christ. I felt much cleaner than I ever had.

"Yet the thing that will always stick with me were the tears in Daddy's eyes as he watched me. He was not overtly emotional, but just about anything to do with his family and the Lord instantly brought tears to his eyes. I think his eyes told me that I had done the right thing. When I looked into them I always sensed that I was seeing a reflection of God's reaction to what I had just done."

For Pat the most important decision of his life had been made. From there he moved on to high school, where he was a gifted athlete, student, and journalist. He also became more and more involved in church work, leading the singing in Church of Christ meetings throughout the area. During this time of worship through song, he realized just how much music meant to him. Through music he truly felt the Lord's Spirit and grace.

After graduation and a year of college, he married his high school sweetheart, Shirley, who happened to be the daughter of the famous gospel singer Red Foley. With his bride at his side, he went back to school, worked in radio, won a couple of national talent searches, earned a record contract, and in four fully packed years became a huge entertainment star and an American hero. Yet through all of this, the moral fiber of the young man didn't change. He remained true to the Christian concepts he had learned from his father, and he continued to constantly read and study the Bible.

Like his father, Pat soon had a large and hungry family. And also like his dad, the entertainer made sure his four daughters' lives were filled with the same devotion to the Word as his early life had been. He thus became a role model for Christian parents everywhere, and he took the responsibility that went with this unexpected position very seriously.

More and more, Pat was asked to share his views. His circle of Christian friends was expanding to embrace many people who loved the Lord, those who had felt the full measure of His grace but were not of the same denomination he was. As he got to know these people, he couldn't see how their salvation experience was any less real than his own. This created questions for which he didn't have ready answers. So, looking to his father's example, Pat sought answers in the Bible and through prayer.

Pat's study caused him to question certain things he had been taught. To answer these questions he returned to the Bible, even studying the Scriptures in Greek. Deciding he didn't have all the answers but that his original viewpoints about salvation had been too limiting, he recommitted his life to Christ. Through his study he had come to the conclusion that believing in Christ as one's Savior was what really mattered, and that the experience of being "baptized in the Holy Spirit" provided the power to live the complete Christian life.

When Pat shared his views with Archie Boone, the older man didn't understand how Pat could possibly think this way. He could not believe that his son would depart from the doctrinal lessons of his youth. Yet, rather than debate his son, the old scholar returned to his own Bible and began to study it. He was bound and determined to bring his son "back into the fold." Together, father and son referenced Bible verses and took a closer look at the workings of the Holy Spirit.

Archie Boone had always welcomed discussions in Sunday school. He had spent years preparing to answer any and every question a student could possibly ask. He had defended his faith more times than he could remember. Now, as he dug into the book he knew so well in order to present the truth to his own son, he found himself locked in a dilemma. The more he read, the more he became convinced that Pat was right.

Archie could have shared these insights with his son and left it at that. If he had, no one would have questioned him and he would have been involved in no controversies. But he didn't. Once he became convinced that his son was headed in the right direction, once he had confirmed through his own Bible study that his long-held beliefs had been too limiting, he let his fellow elders know about his new convictions.

As he stood in the large church he had designed and helped build, he explained his position. He felt he had no choice. He had lived his life as a Christian man, impressing upon each member of his family, as well as all those he had taught in Sunday school, to seek God and His will for their lives every day. He had never backed down from what he believed, and he had raised his children to be just as strong and honest. He now felt he had to speak, to share his discoveries about the reality of the Spirit of God in today's world.

"It was incredible that Daddy was able to take a fresh look at Scriptures he had been studying for a lifetime," Pat said with more than a little awe. "When he did that, he was able to see that the same God who gave such joy to the first-century Christians can still bring such great spiritual joy today. He can still work miracles, and we can't limit Him or draw a line. By doing so we deprive ourselves and others of the real joy of an exciting, Spirit-filled life. The fact that he stood up in front of his own church and told them what he believed, knowing that it would probably cost him his membership, showed just how strong his convictions were. He took a long, strong step of faith."

Archie Boone was more than just the father of an entertainment superstar. He was a man who taught his son that Bible study and growth are not just for the young, that knowing what and why you believe is not just for pastors, and that Christ opens not only hearts but also minds to seek Him. And even if they never met Pat's father, certainly the millions that have come to know more about Christ through Pat Boone's work have been deeply touched by the heart, soul, and vision of Archie Boone.

4

Living by Faith While Playing by the Rules

Bobby Bowden

Florida State University Football Coach

Today, in the game of life, centuries of honored rules are often discarded. The behavior on playgrounds, at sporting venues, and in the business place now embraces such concepts as win by any means, glory without honor, or cheat but don't get caught. Sportsmanship has seemingly become a part of history, and the phrase "the way you play the game" has taken on a meaning unknown a generation ago. Leaders in every occupation, as well as the media and even parents, seem to preach this new winning formula in everything they do.

In a world seemingly driven mad by the bloodlust for victory, Florida State University football coach Bobby Bowden stands apart. He is what is now called old school. He loves to win, but he wants to achieve his goal by playing within the tight and time-honored rules of the game. His devotion to doing it the right way extends beyond the gridiron and to every facet of life itself. Why the man is adamant in his adherence to being a moral leader at a time when morals seem to matter little, if at all, can be traced back more than seven decades to a small home in Birmingham, Alabama.

In the 1930s the Great Depression ran over millions of Americans with the force of an all-American fullback hitting a junior high tackle. No longer was life a game; it was a struggle that pitted mere survival against death, hope against despair, and dreams against nightmares. The sudden downturn of the economy wiped out every fiber of security many families had. While losing almost everything they had worked years to obtain, millions also lost faith.

In a modest Alabama home, a family of four pulled together to beat the odds. The Bowdens scrimped and saved. They ate leftovers and patched and repatched clothes. Like everyone they had their share of doubts, but they never departed from their faith. In fact, when money was short, it was faith that sustained them.

It didn't make any difference if it was a hot and humid summer Sunday morning or a cold and rainy winter Wednesday night. Each time the doors opened at the Ruhama Baptist Church, the Bowdens were there. And they did more than just attend; they were involved. If a voice was needed in the choir, a Bowden became part of the team. If a teacher was needed for Sunday school, then the folks at Ruhama Baptist knew there was always a Bowden who could be depended on to accept the challenge. When the offering plate was passed, even when times were the leanest, the Bowdens contributed their tithe. This kind of faith was so ingrained in their two children that Bobby scarcely remembers not knowing how important it was to be a Christian.

"I can hardly remember not being a believer," Bobby Bowden recalls. "I was always going to church with my mom, dad, and sister. I was literally raised under that godly influence both at home and church. There was no alcohol and no smoking at our house. That was the way a Bowden was supposed to live. My dad always told me to represent the Bowden name in a respectful manner. I grew to understand that meant living with the highest moral values. I knew that just being a Bowden meant I could not be involved in anything that would reflect badly on our name. And, as we were Christians, I also realized from an early age I had to represent the family of God as well."

The Bowdens lived their faith in ways that were obvious. Not only was church the center of their social world but Bible reading and family prayer were a part of their daily lives. Yet beyond the visible elements of faith, Bob and Sunset Bowden displayed the rules of life's game in every one of their actions. Foremost they were always honest, straightforward, and direct. They didn't cut corners, and they believed the only way to do any job was the right way. This kind of living example had an effect on how their son lived and how he believed.

"When I was eleven," Bobby explained, "I was sure the Lord had died to save me, so I walked the aisle at church. I was baptized and joined the church at that time. Oh, I did not have a full understanding of being saved by grace, but I believed that Christ had died for my sins. I also believed that because I was a Christian I now had to be really good. And I tried my best too."

Bobby's church offered a wide variety of activities that encouraged his spiritual growth. From Bible classes, to youth programs, to vacation Bible school, Bobby was immersed in a lifestyle that existed to teach the rules of a Christian life. Ironically, at this time those rules were being challenged, not just on a personal level, but also on a worldwide stage.

At about the time Bobby declared he was a believer, the Japanese bombed Pearl Harbor. The news of the attack and the declaration of war that followed filled millions of Americans with doubt. Within weeks of December 1, 1941, our men were fighting on two fronts, and the odds appeared long. Thousands were dying each day, and some of the dead were well known in the small Ruhama Baptist Church. So despite the fact that life in Birmingham appeared to be fairly normal, it was hard for even children like Bobby to escape the cloud the war had cast over the nation.

It seemed that the very basis of morality was being tested both at home and on the fronts. For many the sneak attack and the horrid news of battlefield casualties made the rules of the past void. Yet in the Bowden house, Bob and Sunset still taught their children the lessons learned in the Bible. Forgiveness and honor remained important, and the couple stressed that victory could be attained without sacrificing one's principles. Even as his father tossed a football around with Bobby, he subtly reminded him victory meant nothing unless it was earned with honor. At the time Bobby was too young to really understand what these lessons meant to global conflict, but he did grasp what they meant in the games he played with his friends.

"I loved athletics," Bobby recalled. "From the time I was a little guy I played baseball, basketball, track, and football."

For Bobby and his family, the games he played in grade school and junior high were an escape. They offered the Bowden family a chance to forget about friends who were caught in the clutches of the war and focus on the joy of playing and watching the drama of sport. It was a time when only what was in front of their eyes mattered. Thus for a few hours each week, Bobby's games muted the news from overseas. Yet even in those days, in games that were far from the national stage, his parents always reminded their son that he was representing more than just himself on the field; he was representing his family and his faith. As one of the city's best athletes, he represented both very well. Yet the significance of scoring a touchdown or stealing a base would soon pale in comparison to the challenge facing the budding star.

By the middle of World War II, in the blink of an eye, Bobby went from racing across grass-covered fields to lying flat on his back fighting for his life. Out of nowhere an invisible opponent took him down.

"When I was thirteen," Bobby explained, "I got rheumatic fever. It was bad. I had to drop out of school, and I couldn't play sports anymore."

Almost unknown today, rheumatic fever was fairly common during the forties. As in Bowden's case, the disease usually began with a sore throat. At first it just seemed like a nuisance, something that slowed Bobby down and caused him to feel lethargic. Yet after several weeks, a serious inflammatory condition began to invade the boy's heart, joints, and nervous system. Some cases of the fever were quickly put to rest, but Bobby's illness developed into a monster.

The doctors treating the boy assured his mother and father he was strong enough to live through the episode. Yet the family was warned Bobby's active days were probably behind him. Rheumatic fever as bad as Bowden's usually caused great damage to heart valves. Because the boy's most vital organ would likely suffer irreversible injury, the best-case scenario had Bobby never again setting foot on an athletic field, and the worst scenario would see him living the rest of his life as an invalid. This was an almost impossible diagnosis for the Bowdens to accept.

For six months the junior high student never left his bed. He had no energy and little fight. In fact, probably the only thing giving the boy the strength to survive was his mother.

"Every time I woke up," Bobby recalled, "Mother was always standing there. Every day she stayed there by my bed. She hand-fed me and, as I could not get up, dealt with my bedpan. She gave up everything for me."

Naturally Bobby was depressed. The world that had once been an extremely bright place was now very dark. His whole life had been turned upside down. In a matter of days he had gone from being an outgoing teenager who was constantly surrounded by friends—an always-on-the-go kid who was involved in everything—to a helpless prisoner locked in a tiny room of his home.

On one of his bleakest days, a time when the teen doubted he would ever get well enough even to walk again, his five-foot-one-inch mother, her gray eyes somehow alive with hope, turned to him and asked a question, "Bobby, do you believe in prayer?"

His eyes never leaving hers, the bedridden lad nodded his head.

"Then be sure to tell Him what you want, and God will hear you."

As the boy stared into his mother's eyes, he saw the Lord looking back at him. Suddenly he believed that God could cure him. He believed that prayers were answered. And he believed that even a sick boy could say a prayer that would touch the highest reaches of heaven.

Bobby began to pray with a fervor he had never before embraced. He asked for his health and strength, he prayed to once again be able to go to school, play sports, and enjoy the beauty of the world around him. He asked the Lord to allow him not to be a burden to his mother. As he prayed, his mother, her eyes glowing, couldn't help but smile. Somehow she sensed that everything was about to be all right.

Not long after that prayer, the teenager not only recovered; he came back faster and stronger than before. By high school he was excelling in every athletic endeavor Woodlawn High offered. From the stands, his mother watched with pride as her son knocked in winning runs, scored touchdowns, and tossed in baskets. By the time he was a senior, the course had been set. Bobby was going to take his game to the next level.

For a boy from Alabama there was only one place to go to college: the University of Alabama. There, the young man who should have been permanently sidelined by rheumatic fever became the team's freshman quarterback. Yet even though playing for the Crimson Tide was a dream come true, the young man was not happy. He felt his life was lacking something. Once again his mother had the answer.

"My mother gave me a book written by Billy Graham," Bobby explained. "It was the first book Billy Graham wrote, and it really got to me."

The young man read *Peace with God* over and over again. He all but memorized the pages, embracing the importance of the words he discovered on them. Through the book he realized that living his human dreams would not bring him the joy he sought. To really be happy he would have to find a way to live out the life God had planned for him.

"Later, when I finally got to meet Billy Graham," Bobby recalled, "and I looked in his eyes, I saw the same thing that I saw in my mother's eyes. Christ was there looking back at me. Since that first meeting I have prayed many nights, asking that God would help me to communicate like Billy Graham."

The first thing Bowden needed to fulfill his role in the "game of life" was a change. In a move that shocked many, the young man left the University of Alabama, returned to Birmingham, and married his high school sweetheart, Ann Estock. Then Bobby restarted his education at Howard College. Not long after receiving his degree and deciding to go into coaching, another realization hit him.

"I discovered that just being good was not enough to be saved. I had not been saved because I was good enough; I had been saved by grace. When I understood that, I really began to grow as a Christian."

Eventually Bobby discovered that his full understanding of grace could be traced back to his mother. She had defined this kind of compassion and sacrifice when he had been sick and bedridden. Through her example she had represented Christ in ways he would appreciate then but did not come to fully understand until later. Her faith gave his life a direction he still embraces to this day.

With the Lord calling the shots, Bowden took a job as the assistant football coach and head track coach at Howard College (now Samford). His next coaching stint took him to South Georgia Junior College. He returned to Samford as head coach in 1959, before landing a position as the wide-receivers coach at Florida State in 1963. In 1966 Bobby moved on to West Virginia, first as the Mountaineer's offensive coordinator, then three years later becoming the school's head coach. In 1976 he accepted the challenge to rebuild the FSU program. Over the next three decades he led the Seminoles to two national championships and fourteen top-five finishes. While adhering to the principles taught to him by his parents, he molded Florida State into one of the most respected football programs in the history of college athletics. Yet few who know Bowden judge him on his amazing record of success on a field. Thanks to the lessons he learned at home, the game of life is where Bobby has really excelled.

He has become a legend off the field for the way he makes time for charity, gives to his church, and reflects Jesus in his twinkling eyes. He greets strangers with a smile. He listens and he cares. His mother would be proud that the words most often used to describe Bobby are *respect, sincerity, class, honesty, charisma, charm,* and *humor.* He thus maintains the integrity of the Bowden name in all that he does. Almost every Sunday morning Bobby stands in a pulpit and points out that football is not the most important thing in the world. He tells countless congregations that it is faith that sustains him and his Christian morals that guide his every move.

And like he did that day in his bedroom, Bobby still prays. He prays with the power and drive he first witnessed in his mother's prayers. And Bowden tries to look at others with the compassion and love he always saw in his mother's eyes.

The game of football has countless phrases and sayings that have wormed their way into almost every facet of American culture. One of the best-known phrases is the "Hail Mary," a last-second pass that has little chance of succeeding without a great deal of divine intervention. There is no biblical record stating the Lord cares about who wins sporting games, but there is plenty of written evidence that the Lord cares a great deal about his people. Bobby Bowden's mother reflected faith in that God when she convinced a sick boy to ask for a miracle, and it happened. With that Hail Mary completed, the game of life gained a coach who has always played by the rules—both on and off the field.

5

All She Needed and More

Karen Kingsbury

Award-Winning Christian Author

Two decades ago, most people who met Karen Kingsbury would have believed she had it all. The California blond drove a red convertible; covered glamorous professional teams like the Los Angeles Lakers, the Los Angeles Dodgers, and the Dallas Cowboys for a daily metropolitan newspaper; and moved in the same circles as many of the movers and shakers in Los Angeles business and society. She was living a dream and, at least at that moment, felt like she needed nothing else to make her life complete. Why shouldn't she have felt that way? Life had presented this young writer with very few roadblocks.

Karen knew she wanted to be a writer from the time she was five years old. At that tender age she penned a book entitled *The Horse*. This was a modest beginning for what would become a very remarkable career.

"I knew I wanted to be a writer the way other children know they want to dance or play sports," Karen recalls. "It was something I was born with."

She wrote all through elementary, junior high, and high school, not only becoming the star of her schools' newspapers and magazines but winning numerous writing awards in state contests. The awards and success continued at Pierce Junior College and at Cal State University, Northridge. At Northridge her stellar work earned her the opportunity to intern in the sport's department of the famed *Los Angeles Times*. She moved on from there, and by the late 1980s Karen's byline was familiar to every reader of the *Los Angeles Daily News*. She was, in a very real sense, a media star.

As was often the case, after work one bright sunny day, Karen made a trip to a Los Angeles health club. The trendy exercise facility was one of the primary social outlets in the city, one of the hot places where singles hooked up and relationships were born. That meant it was also the center for a lot of shallow talk and overused pickup lines. Therefore when a six-foot-two-inch blond-haired man ambled over to her workout station, the writer expected to find nothing but an empty shell under the good-looking package. What she got was not even close to what she expected.

"We had a friend in common," Karen recalled, "so he knew who I was and that I was a sportswriter. At first I thought that was the reason he had come over to talk to me. Yet the more I studied him, the more I saw something I had not seen in other guys. He seemed to have depth, peace, and integrity; those facets made him seem different."

As Karen visited with the man, she discovered he was a former athlete, a model, and a struggling actor. He was back in school now but had not given up on any of his dreams. The gym was full of has-been jocks, starving models, and wannabe stars, so these particular personal elements hardly made him any different than anyone else in the club that day. Yet he was different in that his dreams were coached by his faith, and his faith worked its way easily into his conversation. At that moment this "God talk" made Karen a bit uneasy.

"I think back and wonder, what if I had written him off? The Enemy is so at work in our perceptions, and I could not get past the fact that he loved God and talked about it so freely. That was kind of strange to me. I was a nominal believer in my midtwenties and a member of a major denomination, but I had never opened a Bible to read it. We were very different."

When Don and Karen finished their workouts, he offered to take her home. Though it went against her better instincts, she allowed him to do so. As he dropped her off, he asked if he could take her out on a date. That sounded pretty good to the writer until he added, "Do you care if I bring my Bible?" She agreed to go, but when the evening developed into little more than one-sided theological discussions, she spent most of her time looking at her watch and hoping the hours would move much more quickly than they were. Yet, probably because of his blue eyes, Karen gave Don another chance.

"His sister had sent him a Bible," Karen explained, "and she had asked him to read it and then find a church. He was so into what he was reading that he shared verses with me. As he continued, I became more and more irritated. I now know the Lord was using him to confront my complacency, but to me it felt like a conflict. He had all these verses underlined too. At a point when he showed me a verse from 1 Thessalonians, it hit a little too close to home. I took the Bible, threw it on the ground, and broke it in half."

Don picked up the scattered pages, glanced back at Karen, and left.

What have I done? Karen asked herself as he drove off that day. "I couldn't sleep or eat for the next three days. I remembered things Don had told me and would think, *what if the Lord came back?* Yet even as bad as I felt, I could not call him. I wanted to apologize but couldn't."

Karen decided the only way she could really begin to relate to the man she had so hurt was to engage him in a biblical debate. In other words, she had to do some research.

"I didn't even know Christian bookstores existed," Karen explained. "I found one, went in, picked up a Bible and a study book, and carried these heavy books out to the car."

It took very little time for Karen to realize she had many misconceptions about God's Word, His plan, and how to live a Christian life. The more she read, the more she realized that the man she had driven away three days before had an understanding of things she needed to know more about.

"I called Don and apologized. He told me he had been praying for me. He also told me that he was willing to walk away if I thought that was best. I discovered at that moment that Don was so humble, the picture of strength and quiet grace. At that point I saw him in a new light and was amazed by what I saw. We began visiting different churches to find something that we believed."

Over time the relationship developed to the point where Karen was thinking marriage. She was ready for a proposal. She thought it was coming when Don called one night to talk.

"When he called and told me he had to talk to me, I was thinking romantic thoughts. Yet instead of telling me how much he loved me, he said, 'I just want you to know that I'm going to always love God more than you.' I remember thinking as I listened to those words, *Now that is something you wouldn't see written on a Hallmark card.*

"He explained what he meant by telling me that God would always be first for him. He then told me that even though everyone was sleeping together, we couldn't sleep together. He explained that we would have to draw lines. I didn't understand that kind of thinking. I wondered, what was the problem? What was wrong with him? Yet he was adamant in his belief that God would not bless this relationship unless we put Him first."

Don's biblical wisdom was new to Karen, but it drew her like nothing ever had. So dates continued to be a dinner and a Bible study or a movie and a Bible study. Because of this dating pattern, the people they socialized with were active, spiritual Christians. Conversations usually centered as much on God as they did world events. It seemed that everything else paled in significance compared with faith.

For Karen Kingsbury, up-and-coming writer, a person who was on a first-name basis with all of the city's sports stars, Don's friends were a lot different than anyone she had ever met. Before she met Don, God had been so abstract. Now, in a dramatic about-face, the Lord was there even on dates.

After Don and Karen married, life really got interesting. Don was a student and Karen had her job at the paper. The bylines looked great on the front page, but the pay was lousy.

"We lived in a one-hundred-dollar-a-month garage apartment. Actually it was an old nuclear fallout shelter left over from the Cold War. It had no heat or air-conditioning, but it was fun."

Because the couple was young and had few responsibilities, everything seemed wonderful. Don would get up at 4:30 every morning and pray. The young married duo was developing a

relationship filled with grace. They found cheap ways to entertain themselves. It all seemed like a fairy tale, until Karen found
out she was pregnant.

"Don was so happy," Karen recalled. "But I was not. I pointed
out that I was never going to see this child. I was a top feature
writer; I worked long hours. I simply didn't want to be an absentee
parent. Yet with my job that was the reality I was looking at."

Short of cash, uncertain about her own abilities to support
her family and be a good mother, Karen had problems hanging
onto the faith she had developed since she and Don met. Yet
when the frantic young wife looked into her husband's eyes, she
still saw such great peace. Don really believed that God would
take care of them. Even though he was a student and they were
barely getting by on Karen's salary, this soon-to-be father actually believed the Lord could grant Karen her wish to be a stay-at-
home mom as well as provide the money to keep their growing
family secure. His faith was so deep he simply told Karen, "Just
ask God to show you how to make your living at home."

Even as she looked into her husband's calm eyes, Karen
didn't buy his belief that God would suddenly provide a way to
solve their problems. Yet she had little choice but to pray. After
all, the baby would be joining them sooner than either of them
could imagine.

"I was praying doubtfully," Karen recalled, "and Don was
praying faithfully. When I sold a story to *People*, he was excited
and thought it was an answer to prayer. I pointed out how much
the story didn't pay. I informed him that this is not the way to
make a living."

The magazine piece ran the week their daughter Kelsey was
born. With no other options but the newspaper job open to her,

the writer figured her *People* story would be the beginning and end of her freelance career. In fact, with no evidence to the contrary, when the couple's first child came, it seemed that all of Don's prayers had been for nothing. Yet an unexpected phone call caused a bit of optimism to creep into the new mother's heart.

"A literary agent from New York called," Karen remembered. "Here I was with a four-day-old baby, sharing a new apartment with my husband and a friend from Bible study in order to make ends meet, and this call came out of the blue. The agent told me he thought my *People* story would make a great book. He asked me to write a couple of sample chapters and an outline and send it to him."

Karen wondered if writing the proposal would be worth her time. The agent had told her she might get a small advance. She couldn't leave the paper and stay at home with her child for that kind of money. To quit her day job she was going to have to get enough to sustain the family for three years, until Don got out of school. Her salary at the newspaper could do that, but she knew freelance writing couldn't.

"The book deal didn't seem like an answered prayer to me," Karen explained. "Yet Don felt it was going to work. He began to pray for a book deal that would equal what I made at the paper in three years. I knew it was impossible, but Don never doubted it would happen, so I prayed for it too. Six days before my maternity leave was up, the agent called and informed us that there had been a bidding war between different publishers over my book. I was being offered an advance three times my annual salary. Don had actually been praying for just that amount. 'That is so like God,' Don pointed out to me. 'He so specifically answered our prayer.' I quit my job the next day."

Karen's first release was so popular it spawned several other crime dramas. Yet as her family grew, the writer wanted to make another leap of faith. She wanted to pen books that had Christian impact. She felt called to tell stories reflecting the faith Don had brought to her life and the same faith she now embraced every day. In a real sense, she wanted readers to see Jesus in her words like she saw Him in Don's eyes. The fact that she received exactly what she prayed for didn't surprise her as much this time.

A series of books on answered prayers and miracles began this journey to writing that came from deep in her heart. With bestsellers such as The Redemption Series, *Beyond Tuesday Morning*, *Fame*, and *Oceans Apart*, Karen did more than entertain; she brought the joy and rewards of living a faith-driven life to hundreds of thousands of readers. Today, Karen's books are regularly bestsellers, and what's more, her loyal audience reaches far beyond the "Christian" market. Karen is convinced none of this would have happened if she hadn't looked into a believer's blue eyes at a Los Angeles health and fitness center.

Karen and Don still study the Bible, pray for specific needs, and participate in Bible studies. The writer also still sees Christ in her husband's eyes each time he looks at her or reaches down to help or comfort one of their six children. With more than two million copies of Karen's books in print, a CBS Movie of the Week to her credit, a feature film about to hit the big screens, and a legion of fans waiting anxiously for each new release, Karen does have a blessed life. Two decades ago it appeared as though the writer had it all. Now one look into Karen's eyes proves that she really does have all she needs—and so much more.

6

Happy Trails Even When Times Are Tough

Dale Evans Rogers

Legendary Star, Songwriter, and Christian Leader

Author's note: In 1992 I had the honor of visiting with Dale Evans Rogers about the most important Christian influences of her life. It was really the foundation for this book idea. Though Dale has now gone on to be with the Lord, this story and its inspiration live on. I felt it must be shared in this book.

⁓

It had been a long day. The attractive young woman had gotten up early to make it to her classes at a local business school, preparing herself for a position in the workforce. She was fully aware that even with the extra training, finding employment would be next to impossible. The Great Depression had hit, and jobs were few and far between.

Still, she did have talent, and even during the bleakest of times folks needed entertainment. So after she finished her classes, she raced across town to a Memphis radio station to sing on a live variety show. Much more than a job as a stenographer, a career in show business was her dream. Of course these days the chances of her latching on with a top band were slim. Few people really made much money in entertainment, and those who did usually weren't discovered on a radio station in Tennessee. Deep down she knew that hitting the big time, like finding a job in the business sector, was a long shot at best.

As she left the station, the cold wind blowing through her well-worn coat, the world must have felt like a cruel and lonely place. All around her were people whose lives had been shattered by the dismal economic times. It seemed like everyone was praying for help, but God was not paying any attention. Would things ever turn around? Would America ever be the place where dreams come true, a land of faith, hope, and charity? Surely, as she made her way home, she had to wonder.

Walking up to her parents' house, she felt very lonely and tired. Although still in her teens, she was a single mother, abandoned by her husband when their son was just a baby. She was a small-town kid battling for survival in the big city. This petite woman was fighting the odds just to survive, much less prosper. As she opened the door to her parents' modest home, she must have felt as if she were carrying the weight of the whole world on her aching back.

With her days so crowded with work and study and her nights filled with chores and child care, it would have been so easy for her to have given up. No one would have blamed her. Yet what kept her going was the spirit of the very person who would lead her to someday understand God's plan for her life.

As she walked through the small kitchen, she heard the strains of music coming from the radio. Accompanying the tune was the sweetest voice she had ever heard. Tiptoeing toward the bedroom, she watched as her small son, standing straight up in his crib, swayed with the beat as he hummed each note the band played. He grinned as he listened to the music, his eyes bright with expression and his voice filled with happiness. He seemed to be caught up in the magic of the moment, as though he knew in his heart the joy he felt would go on forever.

As she watched, the tired young woman suddenly felt revived. In the angelic voice of a toddler she had once again recognized a promise of hope, a promise that tomorrow would surely be better than today. Racing into the room, she swept her son up into her arms. Giggling, he hugged his mother, holding tightly to her neck, placing his lips to her cheek. Then he pulled his head back and stared at her. For a moment the young mother could have sworn she saw God's love in those sparkling eyes. Her own eyes welling with tears, she whispered a prayer of thanks for this most precious gift she had ever known.

For most people it would seem difficult to believe that Dale Evans Rogers, who will probably always be remembered as the "Queen of the West," could have ever been in such a dismal situation. Few stop to consider the hard times she went through before she became one of this nation's most beloved and cherished stars. Yet for most of Dale's early life, things were far from idyllic. Day-to-day existence was an unrelenting struggle. The hills she climbed were steep and high, and the doors on which she knocked rarely opened. Long before she was a star, she was a poor unknown girl just battling to survive.

Facing life as a single parent, coming from a background of poverty, trying to make a place for herself during the Great Depression—such circumstances would have been enough to make most people give up before they even got started. But not Dale. She faced the challenges, took them on, and lived a dream. What got her there was hard work, a deep faith, and the love of a wonderful, heaven-sent child.

"When I was about three years old," Dale explained, "I knew that Jesus loved me. My mother taught me that, and I grew up with that concept. That was my foundation."

Dale's mother was a woman of very strong convictions. Like her daughter, she was petite and pretty. She believed in telling the truth at all times no matter what the cost, she believed in following the Bible, and she believed in the power of prayer. She was strong but also soft-spoken. A faithful member of the local Baptist church, she was the kind of woman who always counted her blessings. And, perhaps more than anything else, she was a mother whose love and devotion didn't stop when her child grew up and got married. No matter the time, no matter her little girl's age or position, when her daughter was in pain, she was right there. Dale knew that regardless of her needs, she could rely on her mother to be there for her.

Dale's parents lived in Texas and Arkansas before moving to Memphis to help Dale with her son. It was here in this city with such a long and intriguing musical history that the newly divorced mother attempted to put her life back together. Without her parents' help, Dale probably would have never been able to rebound and develop the vocal talents that would one day make her a star. Without their faith and moral support, she might have had to give up on her dreams of a better life for her son, Thomas, and herself.

"Essentially, my mother and my father raised my son," Dale recalled. "After I began to get more jobs singing, I was traveling a great deal. I worked Chicago, Dallas, Louisville, and several other places both on radio and with bands. Of course I couldn't take him with me, so they would see after him. Still, no matter where I was, no matter how long I would be gone, he was always a light unto my path.

"Even from an early age, he was a very sensitive, musical boy. He learned to sing before he learned to talk. He had perfect pitch. I remember watching him when he was eight or nine years old. My folks were living in Italy, Texas, at the time. On Sunday afternoons, instead of going out and playing ball with the other kids, Thomas would listen to the Boston Pops Symphony on the radio, and he would have two pencils which he would use to 'direct' the orchestra. It was a joy watching him. Even then I could tell that he was truly touched by God."

Dale worked hard and long, and success eventually came. As the years passed, Dale became a local celebrity, and people began to ask for her autograph. Eventually, Hollywood called. Life in show business now offered a great deal of excitement and glamour for this young woman. Yet even though her son was back in Texas living with her parents, Thomas continued to be the most important thing in Dale's life. Her son was her rock, the one who helped her keep her priorities straight.

"I could always see the Lord in him, and he'd been my anchor. After I moved to Hollywood, he came out to live with me. Because he was such a fine Christian, such a great witness, he was my light, the light unto my path. I could see in him all the things I needed to be, all the things I wanted to be."

About this time Dale met a man who would eventually become the love of her life. Roy Rogers was already a superstar. He was a hero looked up to by millions of American children, adored by fans all around the world. Yet he too was lonely. Like Dale, he was a single parent. His wife had died just after giving birth to their son, Roy Jr. Drawn by their common bonds of single parenthood and loneliness, Dale and Roy found themselves spending more and more time together both on the screen and off. And soon, to the delight of Western fans everywhere, the "King of the Cowboys" and the "Queen of the West" were married. Together, they formed a union that would see both great triumphs and great tragedies. Dale believes that the reason their marriage blossomed is because of their faith in the Lord. A faith she never forgot because of her son, who would even make Dale come to church with him on Sunday mornings.

"Right after Roy and I were married, through my son's influence I made a full commitment to the Lord. I gave my life to Christ, holding nothing back. I just let Him have my life and make it what He wanted it to be. Roy also accepted Christ and committed his life shortly after I did.

"When people ask me to what I attribute my success in the movie industry and in my marriage, I always answer that it's because we're Christians, and we understand that our Creator has a plan for every life, and that when we yield ourselves to Him and study His Word, we understand what makes for a good life. We don't have a life where we are always grasping at something beyond our reach, but a life of gratitude to God for the privilege of living and for the privilege of any talent we might have.

"If we are His children, He sees that everything works together for good. In the final analysis, I give Him full credit for our marriage, because we have had many, many sorrows and health problems, but we've always remained firm in our belief in His will for our lives. We lost three of our children, but our faith is stronger today because we never looked back. We always looked ahead."

There can be little doubt that Thomas's faith and influence kept his mother's eyes focused on God. Watching him walk with the Lord encouraged her to find the same kind of direction and faith for her own life. Without her son's influence, Dale might never have become one of this era's most-read Christian authors. She and Roy might never have become one of this nation's most inspiring couples. She also might never have met one of her own mentors and role models, a Sunday school teacher named Henrietta Mears. Thomas was the one who introduced them.

"Henrietta Mears was a spinster lady whose fiancé died when she was about twenty. She was a marvelous Christian. She decided that since God had allowed her fiancé to leave her, she was to be God's handmaiden. In other words, she was to be His bride. She went into the ministry and she owned a gospel press here in Los Angeles which furnished Sunday school materials to churches all over the world. Miss Mears also taught the college and career class at Hollywood Presbyterian Church.

"One time, Tim Spencer of the Sons of the Pioneers asked, 'Miss Mears, don't you miss being married?' She replied, 'No, I am the handmaiden of the Lord, and I am never lonely because He is always with me. Tim, I have about three hundred children, and they are scattered all over the face of the earth as ministers and missionaries.' And she did, too!"

In Henrietta Mears, Dale saw a role model for all Christian women. Mears possessed great love and understanding, and she seemed to be able to forgive anyone's mistakes, overlook their flaws, and see the good. In the midst of her own tragedy, this woman had found great blessings. She had turned death into life, and she had touched thousands.

"She had a real burden for people in show business, and she formed our first Hollywood Christian group. Under her leadership and outreach, people who had been raised as Christians and had gotten away from it got back in the church and grew close to the Lord. She was such a wonderful witness. She never frowned on anybody, and she never looked down on anyone. She was a great influence in my life, next to my mother and my son. She was the most marvelous, giving, wonderful Christian I had ever met.

"I will never forget her funeral. I think she was seventy-three years old when she died in her sleep. Her funeral was the most joyous thing I have ever attended. Nobody shed a tear for her because they knew she was with her Lord. They had a hundred-voice choir, and they sang the 'Hallelujah Chorus' and 'A Mighty Fortress.' It was the most wonderful, the most heartwarming, joyous, victorious funeral I have ever attended, and everybody smiled and was happy for the teacher. She had gone home, but not before she had touched so many."

How important was it that Henrietta Mears had come into Dale's life? For millions of Americans it was vital. Because of Mears's example, Dale Evans Rogers turned one of her own tragedies into one of the greatest triumphs in Christian literature. *Angel Unaware*, the story of Dale and Roy's baby with Down syndrome, is one of the most widely read and distributed books in our time. Now in its twenty-ninth printing, the story of Robin's life has revealed the specialness in all of God's children.

This one book, whose profits have always gone to special-needs organizations, has done more than raise money. It has raised the level of the collective American consciousness. A once shunned and hidden segment of our society saw doors begin to open wide. Suddenly, men and women began to see the potential of those who were once automatically shuffled off to state hospitals to await an inevitable death. Because of Dale's inspiring book, changes were made, research was done, and medical advances were accomplished. Now, millions of angels like Robin are active in the workforce, lead normal lives, and even star on television shows. All of this is due in large part to Dale's seeing what the world would call a tragedy as one of God's greatest gifts. And she learned how to do this through a woman she met because of her son Thomas.

Dale loved to talk about her son. "Not long after Thomas came to join me in Hollywood, he met a girl who became his wife. They formed a team. She is his organist and pianist, and they have been in Christian ministry all of these years. They have been such models, both of them, and they have three Christian daughters. Today, Thomas is a minister of music. He has been all his adult life. He has a master's degree from the University of Southern California."

When Dale talked about her son, her voice revealed more than just a mother's love and pride. It was obvious that she believed this boy was a gift sent to her to make sure she recognized the power of her Lord. From those first moments when she thought times were at their darkest and the future looked so bleak, to the time when she became one of this nation's most treasured celebrities, Dale Evans Rogers continued to look into her son's deep brown eyes, always seeing the love of her Lord—a love that has changed the world through Dale's life.

7

A Servant's Heart

John Cathcart

President of World Missionary Evangelism

The sun was bright, but the world seemed darker than it had ever been. John Cathcart, who just a year before had been a high-paid engineer with a corner office in a North Dallas high-rise office tower, was now nervously walking down a dusty path in the vast Kenyan slum of Kibera. In this horrid place there was no power or water, and raw sewage flowed down and across the narrow, heavily rutted streets. Even John's highly trained scientific mind could not begin to comprehend that a million people lived within a few square miles of where he walked, and all of them were desperately poor. John studied the tiny huts that were sandwiched one on top of the other, looking more like trash heaps than houses. In those tin and cardboard shacks children huddled together, trying to avoid being the latest victim of the thousands of human predators who roamed Kibera. Yet when they spied the American, when they heard his unique accent as he spoke to his wife, a handful of these small victims of poverty, mostly naked, sick, and hungry, nervously made their way out into the sunlight to catch a glimpse of this unique visitor. To them the white-haired stranger might offer a chance for a meal, and they would face the devil himself to get a bite to eat.

It took a lot of courage for one small youngster to approach John. Shooing away the flies that were attacking the sores near his eyes, the boy raced up to the man and hopefully held out his hands. Cathcart studied the child for a moment, smiled, then reached into his pocket and pulled out a candy bar. The boy giggled and grabbed it. Suddenly twenty more children followed the first one's example and ran up to John, but there was nothing left for them.

As he observed the disappointment in the children's eyes, John wondered why he had bothered coming into this hell on earth. With so many helpless and hopeless people all around him, how could he possibly do anything for them? Yet because of the impact his father had made on his life, rather than turn and go back to his hotel, he continued to walk and pray.

John Cathcart was born in Australia. He came to the United States at the age of twenty. After earning a degree in chemical engineering, John began a stellar career working for some of the largest engineering firms on the globe. Through his jobs he traveled all over the world. Yet no matter where he was, thanks to his upbringing, he remained active in every facet of the church. Even as a layman he became a powerful teacher and preacher.

By his late sixties John had everything he could have possibly wanted. He was respected as both a professional engineer and a Christian, but there was still an unexplained emptiness in his heart. One day he was staring out his office window contemplating his future when his phone rang. It was someone from World Missionary Evangelism, a Dallas-based organization involved in Christian relief programs in Third World nations. One of the founders of the mission had died, and they needed a new president. The board of directors wanted to know if John might consider taking the position.

Cathcart should have been thinking about retirement, not about embarking on a new career. Besides, the demands of this new job were great, while the salary wasn't. On top of that he had no experience in this mission. Yet the call would not leave him alone. As he would later tell his wife, "Always being active in the church sometimes does not satisfy the cry that is in our soul." It was a cry he knew his father had heard too. Over the next few weeks that cry, like it never had before, seemed to demand that John follow in the footsteps of his father, William Cathcart.

"It is not so much that I saw Jesus in his eyes," John explained as he remembered how much his father's influence affected his decision to take this new challenge, "but that I saw Jesus *through* his eyes. This may be an unusual statement, particularly in these days and times when so many parents don't set good examples for their children, but he was a very unusual man and a great example as a parent. In truth, I didn't realize that until I was grown." And perhaps John didn't really understand the full impact of his father's life until the moments when he mulled over taking the top position at World Missionary Evangelism.

William Cathcart had been born in Scotland, but when his mother died during his youth, his father shipped the boy to the north of Ireland to live with his aunt. Along with his five siblings, he was for all practical purposes an orphan. Life was anything but easy for this hand-me-down group. About the time William finished high school, World War I broke out. In his four years on the western front, the young man was involved in some of the fiercest and largest battles of the war. He even watched his brother die of mustard gas poisoning. Toward the end of the war William was so badly injured that he was placed in a hospital for incurable soldiers.

"My father didn't know the Lord at this time," John explained, "but the Lord appeared to him and told him he was going to raise him up and give him a shepherd's heart, then send him to the outermost parts of the earth. My father had no idea what a shepherd's heart was, but he would soon find out. In time, when he had recovered enough, the administrators would let him out of the hospital for a few hours each day. On one of those trips he met Andrew Turnvull. Turnvull was a renowned pastor whose church was called the Burning Bush."

In his quest to understand the meaning of a shepherd's heart, William began to go to Turnvull's church. There he accepted the Lord as his Savior and, at about the same time, saw his health return. Fully recovered, he took a job in sales during the day and at night became a student of the Bible. In the pages of his Bible the young man scribbled notes and underlined verses as he searched for his destiny. First as a teacher, then as a pastor, William eased into that destiny. After preaching in Ireland, Scotland, Wales, and England, all the time looking for the Lord's will for his life, William felt a call to the South Pacific. Gathering up his family, he began a mission to Australia, New Zealand, and Tasmania with little more than a well-worn Bible and a prayer. This quest brought into tight focus his shepherd's-heart dream.

"Though it was the middle of the Great Depression, he refused to be paid by the denomination that sent him," John recalled. "In Australia he founded a tea company and supported his ministry and family with that business. That is just the way he was.

And God wonderfully blessed him in Australia, where more than seven hundred churches were raised up under his leadership."

In 1950, after successful missionary work in both the South Pacific and South Africa, William resigned as a missionary and came to the United States. He was now old enough to retire and turn over the hard work of spreading the good news to a younger generation, but he didn't. In his new home he traveled extensively, teaching and preaching from coast to coast and border to border. During this time his son began to see the retired missionary as someone special.

Because John had been born after William's missionary work had begun, he had taken his father's Christian service for granted. Now, as an adult, he began to realize how different William was from normal men. As John analyzed why his father stood head and shoulders above everyone else he knew, the younger Cathcart grew to understand it all came down to faith. In every facet of his father's life, John saw the Lord at work.

John explained, "The first way in which I saw God through my father's eyes was in his life or in his walk. There is an expression today, 'They can talk the talk but they can't walk the walk.' This man was a hundred percent committed to God and to the work of God. I never saw him in any way conduct himself privately that he could not also conduct himself publicly. He was such a success in his work for God that it was very, very impressive.

"The second way I saw God through his eyes was in his preaching. He was described by many as the greatest Bible teacher they had ever heard. His preaching was absolutely mind-boggling. I have seen him take a Scripture such as Isaiah 6 and preach on that for six weeks, six nights a week. The entire time he held people spellbound. God's presence filled his life and ministry, and that gets your attention.

"The third way I saw the Lord through his eyes was in his prayer life. This man could pray! It was quite an experience to be in a prayer meeting with him. A woman in Scotland who had known him as a young minister once told me that when he prayed in a house, it felt as if the furniture moved. I would say this: if it didn't move, it should have moved. His prayers were not wild or off the wall, but they had a weight and depth that touched realms and dimensions in God that most of us never know about.

"The fourth way I saw God through his eyes was in his talk. Just the way he knew God and the way he knew the Word of God, and his vast experiences—it was just remarkable. To listen to him tell you about the Lord was mesmerizing.

"And the fifth and final way that I saw the Lord through him was in his Bibles. I remember coveting this man's Bibles. I set out to get as many of them as I could. He went through them like people go through notebooks. He would mark them and make notes in them. You could get an education just reading his notes on the book of Psalms or on other passages of Scripture."

"There was one Bible he had I really wanted," John recalled. "My father knew that and finally gave it to me for a birthday present. I watched as he wrote a word of dedication in the front of the book. I was very interested to see what it was he would write. In a Bible you would expect Scripture or something deep and profound. Instead he used a quote from the poet Robert Browning."

And so I live, you see,
Go through the world, try, prove, reject,

Prefer, still struggling to effect
My warfare; happy that I can
Be crossed and thwarted as a man,
Not left in God's contempt apart,
With ghastly smooth life, dead at heart,
Tame in earth's paddock as her prize.

"As I read those words from the poem 'Easter,' I realized this is the way my father lived. He would rather live a life of challenges and uncertainty than play it safe."

Decades after first reading those words, John found himself in an African slum wondering why the Lord had sent him to such a dark place. His wife, who was by his side that day, would later say, "You could look into the eyes of the men and there was nothing there. There was no life." Neither John nor Patricia had ever witnessed such hopelessness. It was as if this world was void of God.

In the middle of that slum was a piece of property owned by World Missionary Evangelism. From a worldly standpoint it was worthless. Yet as John studied the deserted stone buildings and rocky courtyard, he now saw them as if he was looking through his father's eyes, and he knew William would have seen promise, hope, and the door of opportunity. With that vision in mind, John's heart began to soar. A school and feeding center could be built here, he thought. He knew that while this facility couldn't help all the children of the slum, it could help some. Maybe here, in the middle of the slum, he could give a few of them a future.

Five years later the light has come into the darkness. The center is feeding, clothing, and educating more than eight hundred children.

"My father was in his nineties when he developed cancer," John explained. "He was in hospice care. The woman who was taking care of him saw him as a ninety-five-year-old man. As she watched us gather around him she found it strange we were so well adjusted in what should have been a moment of sorrow. My brother and I explained to her that our father was a giant, a leader, a captain of the church. We knew he had no regrets about his life, and we had no regrets either.

"When we were growing up he would take off and be gone for months with his missionary work. He knew that because of God's call he wasn't the father he really wanted to be. One day he was speaking to my older brother, and he started to apologize for being away from us so much. But then he stopped and said, 'You know, but if I had it to do all over again, I would do the same thing.'"

As a child John Cathcart might not have fully understood his father's thinking, but now he does. John gave up the good life to follow in his father's footsteps. At a time when most men dream of walking golf courses or scouting out fishing holes, John travels the world searching for ways to make a difference for the Lord. Like his father, he is embracing his shepherd's heart.

8

Giving Others What Mother Couldn't Have

Truett Cathy

Businessman

Truett Cathy is a legend in the fast-food business. His Chick-fil-A restaurants are some of the most popular eating spots in the United States. To many, these eateries with their tasty chicken and funny ads define Truett. Yet while it is true that Chick-fil-A brought this businessman his fame and fortune, the principles that have made the family-oriented chain flourish are what reveal the heart of this dedicated Christian man. They are values he learned in a home where his mother toiled seven days a week, three hundred and sixty-five days a year, just to support her children. As Truett's life has proven, she didn't just feed her kids at the table; she also fed their souls with a recipe that insured rich character and deep, lasting faith.

Truett was born on a Georgia farm but grew up in Atlanta. He was the sixth of seven children. Knowing the importance of Christian role models, his mother, Lilla, named her son after the great preacher George Washington Truett. Little did she realize that this Truett would one day not only be as famous as his name-sake but also represent the same kind of Christian commitment.

"Because of the Depression, Father could no longer find work, so Mother became our leader," Truett explained. "To provide for us, Mother turned our home into a boardinghouse. Mother worked like a slave, keeping house and cooking for her seven children and a household of boarders. I never saw her close her eyes in sleep. Not until she lay in her coffin did I see my saintly mother at rest."

Running a boardinghouse was a huge job. Including her family, as many as fifteen people depended upon Lilla's skills as a cook, housekeeper, and negotiator. She had to keep things running smoothly, as well as maintain peace in the house. It was a job that took all of her time, energy, and brainpower.

Even as a very small boy, Truett often worked at his mother's side. As he assisted her with her kitchen chores, he noted her positive attitude and her commitment to work.

"Being brought up in the boardinghouse," Truett explained, "I would often help out. She taught me how to shuck corn, shell peas, prepare dishes, set the table, and shop. I even flipped eggs and pancakes on the grill."

As Truett worked with his mother, he grew to understand she was doing this backbreaking job so the Cathy family could survive. Yet in the midst of these hard times Lilla also unselfishly reached out to others battered by the Depression. Many of her boarders had been forced to give up their old lives, sell all their possessions, and move to the city. Like the Cathy family, they too were scraping by. Most of them did not have any close relatives and were completely alone. The boardinghouse was their last stop before finding themselves on the streets. Therefore many of them were beaten down, brokenhearted, and hopeless.

Lilla reached out to each of them with a caring hand and a gentle spirit. She treated all of them, no matter their shortcomings or faults, with great respect.

As her boarders quickly learned and her children grew to know over time, Lilla reflected her faith in everything she did. She was a role model as both a mother and a woman. She felt it was her duty to make sure her children never missed Sunday school or church. Yet each Sunday the stocky brunette sent her kids off to services with clean clothes but a heavy heart. How she wanted to be there with them. How she wanted to gather with other people her age and worship the Lord. Yet her duties at the boardinghouse did not allow this luxury. And for Lilla, that is what attending worship services were: a luxury.

"I was brought up to go to Sunday school and church," Truett remembered. "My mother was unable to go to church on Sunday because she had to prepare the Sunday meal, and my daddy missed out as well, but Mother made sure I was programmed to go to Sunday school and church."

Just because she was working and could not attend conventional church services did not mean Lilla did not worship. As she prepared her meals and did her housework, she faithfully tuned her radio in to Charles E. Fuller and listened to his *Old-Fashioned Revival Hour*. On Sunday afternoons, after the dishes had been washed, Lilla would adjust her wire-rim glasses, pull out a few old hymnbooks, and play the home's piano. Like clockwork, her children and even some of the boarders would gather around and join her in singing their favorite gospel numbers. These simple actions, along with daily Bible study and prayer, helped her keep her spiritual life focused. It also made a mighty impression on her children. But as sweet as these special moments were, Lilla still longed for the more intimate experience of real church and community worship. Sadly this was something she simply could not have.

By the age of eight, in an attempt to keep his family solvent, Truett had joined the workforce. He bought six-packs of Cokes for a quarter and sold them door to door for a nickel a bottle. Though he then had a terrible speech impediment, he soon branched out and marketed magazines door to door. These business experiences were obviously preparing him for career opportunities down the road, but it would be another experience that placed his whole life into the proper perspective.

"When I was twelve I received Christ as my personal Savior and thus decided who my Master would be," Truett explained. "I felt it was a normal thing for me to do. To this day I thank the Lord I didn't do a lot of things I probably would have done if I hadn't become a Christian at that early age. Being saved was the beginning for me."

His mother was thrilled when Truett accepted Christ. She had prayed for this since before the boy was born. Having him anchored in his faith made her long hours of labor seem easier. Yet even hard work and faith do not always keep a business going. When the Depression grew so difficult that boarders could no longer pay their rent, Lilla had to shut down her boardinghouse. Times then grew so tough she could not even pay her own debts. As she believed being responsible for debts was a matter of Christian principle, she sensed she had failed as a witness and steward of the faith.

Truett knew that owing money bothered his mother a great deal. He was so moved by her need to make her life right, he joined the service and paid off his mother's debts with his own earnings.

To the young man it was not just the right thing to do but a testament to the great sense of moral responsibility implanted in him by Lilla.

After World War II, Truett and his brother opened the Dwarf Grill. The men worked twelve-hour shifts to keep the small eatery running around the clock. The only day they closed was Sunday. Both agreed that being in church was more important than making a few extra bucks. Just as the business was beginning to take root, Truett's brother was killed in a plane crash. Truett somehow found the strength to continue. In fact, he expanded his work, created a chicken sandwich, and in the process changed the fast-food world. But even as he found success, Truett continued to reach out to those needing a helping hand. The more success he had, the more it seemed he wanted to give back.

"A man in the restaurant business is almost like a ministry in itself," Truett explained. "In this business you have the ability to furnish food, serving people and meeting their physical needs and most spiritual needs. I do feel it is a ministry that the Lord has given to me. In the Bible there are many stories of the wonderful experiences with Jesus Christ around the dining table."

Truett carried his principles over to the way he treated employees. Eddie White started working for Truett at the Dwarf Grill in 1948 when he was just twelve years old. A few years later White, the oldest of seven children from a very poor family, felt he had to drop out of school in order to provide for his brothers and sisters. To prevent this from happening, Truett reworked the young man's schedule, gave him a raise, and even allowed him to use his own car. The next year when it came time for Eddie's high school prom, Truett paid for it. The fact that this was pre-integration Atlanta, Georgia, and White was African-American did not stand in the restaurant owner's way. Thanks to his mother, he saw all people as his family.

In a sense, each of Truett's business principles were learned at the boardinghouse. Without even thinking about it, each step of the way as he built his empire, Truett reflected his mother's compassion, spirit, and faith.

"I have three children," Truett points out with obvious pride, "twelve natural grandchildren, and then I have 135 adopted grandchildren. They are my grandchildren by choice. We have fourteen foster homes, and each home has twelve children. The homes are located in Georgia, Alabama, and Tennessee. My daughter and her husband were missionaries in Brazil for ten years. They told us the country had ten million street children. There was a need, and we felt we had to do something. So we built a home there as well."

The foster homes are set up a bit like Lilla's boardinghouse, with a family environment, a deep-running Christian influence, and a positive atmosphere. Yet Truett's passion for mentoring youth doesn't begin and end with the homes. Like everything in his life, his faith is hands on.

Through Chick-fil-A, Truett has provided hundreds of college scholarships to kids who have worked in his stores. He has established the WinShape Centre to help youth build a foundation for happy and successful lives. Though now in his eighties, Truett continues to teach a boy's Sunday school class at the First Baptist Church in Jonesboro, Georgia.

"I have taught thirteen-year-old boys Sunday school for fifty years," Truett modestly admits. "This age is the last opportunity you have to establish values before the boys hit the critical years. I tell the boys in my Sunday school class, if you want to be an A student, associate with A students; if you want to be an athlete, associate with athletes; if you want to be a winner in anything, associate with people who are winners." Certainly by associating with Truett each week, the kids are coming into contact with one of this country's big winners.

In 2004 Truett traveled to Washington, D.C., to address many of the nation's top elected representatives on business ethics. Truett told the group, "I run my company on biblical principles, and those principles do work. I am convinced the Bible is a roadmap for our lives. We could all do well by following the principles that are taught in the Bible." These were principles that Truett first learned at his mother's side in a boardinghouse.

Remembering back to his days of watching his mother's sacrifice for others, the businessman has done one additional thing in her honor. Truett closes his restaurants on Sundays. He wants all those who work for him to have the chance his own mother did not—to go to church. So in that way, whenever anyone sees a Chick-fil-A closed on Sunday, they are seeing the faith Truett Cathy saw in the heart and eyes of his mother, Lilla Cathy.

9

A Big Man's Strong Example

Charlie Daniels

Country Music Singer

In the early 1940s the very fiber of the United States was shaken to the core. World War II had locked this nation and its people in a battle not just for the survival of the American ideal but for the survival of the very essence of Christian morality. On one continent was an enemy led by a demonic dictator who was killing God's chosen people by the millions. On another continent was a foe whose people actually believed their leader was a living deity. In the middle was a country unprepared for war and depending on the heroism of men who valued peace and goodwill above everything else.

In Wilmington, North Carolina, a tall man with strong features looked into the massive man-made storm that was shaking the entire world with the kind of faith and assurance that calmed all those around him. He remained steadfast in his belief that right would triumph and that those who chose to rise up against goodness would be wiped out. Time and time again, from his days as a craftsman to his years spent carving highways out of bedrock and mountain, to the time he spent in the lumber industry, he had watched Americans take on every challenge and beat the odds. And now, each night as he prayed, he knew that the same God who had so blessed him and countless others around the world would not forget them now. His strong, unwavering faith was an inspiration to those who left to fight as well as to those who were left behind to hope and pray.

Often as this strong man walked the trails around his home, a small boy tramped along by his side. Only five years old, little Charlie Daniels didn't understand why the Germans and Japanese were fighting the United States, nor did he know that countless millions were living in fear as they faced an enemy that seemed to be invincible. All he knew was his grandfather could face down any man, and as long as Granddad was by his side, the boy was safe from even Satan himself.

"I don't think I would have been scared of the devil if he walked up to the front porch as long as my granddad was there," Charlie Daniels laughed. "He was the kind of person who you just felt could handle any situation. No matter how difficult it was, no matter how physical it became, he could do whatever it took to come out on top. When I was a child, and even when I became an adult, I didn't feel like there was anything Granddad was afraid of."

Granddad Grahman was very much a man's man, the most manly person Charlie had ever known. In his younger days he had been quite a rounder. He was a physically strong man, and his feats of strength were legendary. Once he put on his back a bale of cotton weighing over five hundred pounds and walked around a building just to prove he could do it. He was a natural leader, a confident man, the kind of man people listened to and followed.

Still, just because he was strong and able didn't mean that he was cold or uncaring. He was a man of great Christian principles. He was compassionate. If someone had been hurt, he reached out to help them. If someone needed something, he gave it to them. He constantly helped people. He had the biggest, softest heart in the world. His love crossed all lines. He didn't care what color a person was, or what his background was. If somebody needed something, he felt it was his Christian duty to see that he gave it to them.

To this day Charlie has no idea just how much his grand-dad did for people or how many people he helped. No one but his granddad and the Lord know. But Charlie was always over-whelmed by how much his granddad did for people without ever asking for anything in return.

Granddad Grahman's faith inspired more than just his eldest grandson. In times of great doubt and fears, those who worked under him, as well as those who went to a small Baptist church with him, realized that this man's faith was even greater than his physical abilities. In the midst of a world war or times of local and personal grief, this man's man was there offering not only the strength of his arms but the power of his faith.

"My whole family were very strong Christians," Charlie related as he looked back over five decades. Then laughing he added, "My grandmother was so staunch that when we went coon hunting on a Saturday night, if our hunt lasted into Sunday morning, it was wrong. Just like Granddad Grahman, in her mind right was right, wrong was wrong, and you didn't compromise the two. I came up in that kind of environment.

"You know, thinking back, I didn't even know anyone in my young life who was an atheist. I didn't know a single person who didn't believe in God. I didn't even know anybody who didn't believe that Jesus Christ was the Son of God. I didn't know anybody who would speak blasphemy or anything like that. I had heard of people like that, but I didn't know any of them. That is just how I came up. It was just never a question in my life about the reality and power of God."

Many people are raised in an environment where church and the Lord are facts of life. Many folks know about Jesus before they know how to spell their names. Many live in households where family prayer and Bible readings are a part of everyday life. Yet few have a role model that shows his faith, his strength, his heart, and his love like Charlie had in his grandfather.

"He was a remarkable man," Charlie admitted. "He was wise, and even though he didn't have much formal schooling, he was very literate. He could read and understand the King James Version of the Bible. I still have problems understanding it. But he could explain each story, each verse, and he seemed to always recognize God's plan for his life.

"As time went along, probably due to all that he had seen and done, he became more and more spiritual. One of the things that became more and more important to him was family prayer. It was so beautiful to sit there and listen to him pray for his family, to pray for his children and grandchildren. It was just a total inspiration to me."

Being the oldest grandchild, Charlie spent a lot of time with the man who would so shape his young life. In a boat fishing, in the woods hunting, or just on the porch watching the trees, the two of them shared countless hours. Much of that time, Charlie listened intently as his grandfather spoke of the most important things that had happened during his own life.

"In a way he had been a pioneer," Charlie recalled. "He had helped build the roads. It had been hard work, and I loved to hear him talk about it. Yet, more than just his stories, what I really learned from him were his views of life. In his life there were no gray areas. Right and wrong were clearly defined. He was going to do the right thing all the time, not just when it best served his needs. He was also going to stand up for what he believed, not just in church or at home, but everywhere. He didn't care how many people stood up against him. He would fight if that's what it took to back up what he believed. When it came to right and wrong, there was no compromise.

"He also believed first and foremost in what Christ said, 'I give you a new commandment, love one another.' By helping everyone who needed help, whether he agreed with them or not, he did his best to live up to that commandment. He recognized that being a Christian meant you could be both strong and compassionate."

Granddad Grahman was the most direct man Charlie Daniels would ever meet. Because he constantly read the Scriptures, walked with the Lord, and sought to do His will, this robust leader never seemed confused by the negative elements of life. Just as he knew America would win the war, he also knew that a minor crisis at the plant would work itself out when folks pulled together to solve the problem.

"One of the things my granddad taught me," Charlie shared, "is that one of the devil's big tools is confusion. If you are confused, you can't be positive. Granddad took his time and carefully sorted things out. He didn't let a mass of problems build up and cloud his judgment. He turned them over to God and got on with life. He never let anything get in the way of his vision.

"He also had a philosophy that accepted the fact that he wasn't going to be perfect, but by the same token, he felt he sure had to continue to work toward it. So he never quit trying to grow."

Inspired by the stories of men and the mountains, driven by his need to express his own imagination, Charlie grew up to embrace music as a form of expression. This choice inspired the young man to write his first song when he was a teenager and form his first band when he was barely in his twenties. Before he was thirty, he had written a hit for Elvis Presley. Then, six years later, he formed the Charlie Daniels Band, and his career really took off. Hit followed hit, and Charlie gained immense respectability on both the pop and the country sides of the charts. He played before millions, and his band was known as one of the top live entertainment acts in the world. He then embraced Christian music and became one of country music's loudest spiritual voices.

Although things had changed a lot since those carefree times spent walking by his grandfather's side, Charlie himself had not changed much at all. Even when it was not a smart move professionally, he always stood up proudly for what he believed. He wouldn't allow gray areas to cloud his judgment. He drew his conclusions on right and wrong relying on the same biblical truths his grandfather had used. And no matter how famous he became, he never quit going back to visit the old man. The two would sit on the front porch for hours on end and discuss the most meaningful facets of life.

"We had a great rapport. As I grew older I enjoyed him even more. He was a very affectionate person, and I am too. I hug folks. I'm a big hugger. My granddad and my whole family were that way."

One of the most loving acts in the whole world is when a strong man reaches down to gently lift and hug a small child. This action bonds the two and opens the door for an exchange of ideas that can shape a lifetime. Such was the case between Charlie Daniels and his grandfather.

"I loved him very much," Charlie sincerely related. "When he passed away, I missed him, but I couldn't feel bad about his dying. Like the Book says, 'Don't weep for the dying.' He was going to a better place. I knew that, he had assured me of that, and that was enough."

When Charlie's grandfather departed his earthly home at the age of eighty-two, he left a great deal of himself behind not only in the many hundreds of his neighbors he touched with his acts of faith, courage, and compassion but in a grandson who followed him step by step for more than four decades. Without his even realizing it, Granddad Grahman's influence could be felt throughout the world in the actions and songs of his grandson.

"I look back and the thing that stands out the most about him was his compassion," Charlie explained. "I hope that if I inherited anything of his it would be compassion. Also, he could have been judged on his work, his family, and his words. Yet he didn't look for human greatness or recognition; he was just doing what he felt he was supposed to. I think the bottom line was that his life taught me a great deal about what being a Christian means.

"It took me a long time to understand just a little bit about the sacrifices of Jesus Christ, and I am still trying to understand more about them. I just cannot understand that kind of love. But Granddad tried to live it in the way that he helped others. So through Granddad's life, I can understand my Savior a little better."

While Charlie was working on a holiday album, the faith planted by his grandfather came into sharp focus in Charlie's own life.

"I don't know how you can do anything about Christmas," Charlie explained in a strong tone, "and not tell what it is really all about. Christmas is, always was, and always will be about the birth of Jesus Christ. Anything that I have to do with Christmas will emphasize that fact. I did a Christmas album a few years back, and I told them from the first that what I wanted was to write the songs for it. I also wanted to do it at Christmastime so I could experience the real spirit of the moment, and I wanted it to reflect the real spirit of Christmas in every word and message. I feel we accomplished those things in the album and the special, and I thank God for that.

"You see, I couldn't accept something where they would tell me I couldn't talk about my faith during the Christmas season or for that matter any other time. If somebody tells me we can't talk about Christ because a lot of the listeners aren't Christians, then I answer by saying, 'That's not my fault, they should be.' How can you be any other way and live with yourself?"

Charlie Daniels is an entertainment legend. He is the man who musically informed us that "The South Is Going to Rise Again" and that "Simple Men" were the best. In one of his most famous tunes he even looked the devil in the eye and beat him at his own game. He has crisscrossed the nation and circled the globe. He has played before kings and presidents. He has given tens of thousands of hours and countless gifts in an attempt to express his faith. Numerous Christian organizations have honored him for his charity. But more than any of that, what probably thrills him most is when the old folks who attend a small

Baptist church in Wilmington, North Carolina, get together on their front porches or at ice cream socials and say, "Didn't that oldest Daniels boy grow up to be just like his granddad! You can see the old man in the kid's eyes."

When they say that, somewhere, on a farm in Tennessee, a gleam is evident in the entertainer's eye. And somewhere, across a river called Jordan, another big man's eyes are gleaming too.

10

The Importance of the Word

Jerry Burden

Head of Gideons International

Nashville is known across the world as Music City. Men and women from all over the globe flock to this Tennessee community in hopes of landing a recording gig. Each has a dream of being a star so they can take their messages in song to millions. A few make it, sign a record deal, and find themselves on the road performing one-night stands night after night. In city after city these entertainers wander into countless motel and hotel rooms. In these rooms, waiting to offer relief and hope, can always be found one of Music City's other major worldwide exports: the Bible.

Jerry Burden is not a musician, but he did come to Nashville with a dream: to keep the printed Word of God at the top of the world's reading charts. He directs a mission going back more than one hundred years, the well-known Gideons International. How Jerry became the head of Gideons is the story of three unique men who reflected the Lord in their eyes, words, and actions.

Jerry has southern roots. He is a product of the region, a down-home man who grew up in the church. Though he walked the aisle and was baptized at an early age, Jerry's knowledge of the Bible was only what little he had absorbed in Sunday school classes or by listening to sermons. When he graduated from college with an education degree in biology, his knowledge of theology was still elementary, and he saw no need to learn more.

Jerry and his new bride packed up their bags soon after graduation and headed west. In Tempe he began to work on a graduate degree in ecology at Arizona State University. Jerry wanted to use his studies to help save the world from the excesses and destruction brought on by man. He would ultimately live that dream, but in a much different manner than he had planned.

In the late sixties America was awash in new thinking. Many in the baby boomer generation were tired of doing things the same old way. They saw the war in Vietnam, the destruction of many of the earth's natural resources, and the oppression of certain ethnic groups as spiritual causes that demanded action. As much of this thinking was centered on college campuses, Jerry saw the devotion and determination, along with the confusion and frustration, of this new breed of young people. For many in the turbulent sixties, the spiritual quest for answers took folks everywhere but the Bible. At that moment Jerry wasn't looking at God's Word for answers either. Nevertheless, the Bible was about to become the roadmap for the rest of his life.

"When we moved to Tempe," Jerry remembered, "we started looking for a church home. Being Baptist, naturally the first place we visited was First Baptist Church. I remember that morning so well. The church's pastor, Rev. Ernest Laycock, was preaching on Esther. He was going through the book verse by verse. He wasn't just preaching, like I was used to; he was doing a very systematic teaching and showing how the verses related to our everyday lives. I was immediately captivated by what I was hearing."

This was the first time Jerry ever felt Scripture come alive. As the preacher spoke, the words suddenly had impact. Now the Bible was not ancient history; it was a living body of work that meant as much today as it had thousands of years ago. As the young man stared into the eyes of Rev. Laycock, he sensed the presence of the Lord as he never had before. Needless to say, the couple joined and quickly became regulars at every one of the church's services.

"As week after week I listened to Rev. Laycock," Jerry explained, "I felt a need to know more about Scripture. Here was a godly man, a man with a pastor's heart, who lifted Christ up in everything he did, and yet he also had a deep, rich mind. I was simply entranced by him."

As Jerry sensed the special qualities in the preacher, the older man noted something in the grad student as well. He felt a need to reach out to the Burdens, to get them involved in every facet of the church, and to make them feel like family. It seemed Laycock wanted to challenge them, especially Jerry, to grow as Christians. This led to the preacher and his wife inviting the couple to their home for Thanksgiving dinner.

"I was amazed by this man's compassion," Jerry remembered. "And his depth of understanding fascinated me as well. I may have been working on my ecology degree, but because of Rev. Laycock, I was now a lot more interested in the Scriptures than I was in science."

During his years at First Baptist, Ernest Laycock tapped into Jerry's quest for knowledge. This led to intense Bible study, positioning the young man to become an active part of the church's Sunday school program. Yet when the preacher moved on, giving up his pastorate and starting a new chapter in his life, Jerry was worried. He honestly felt there could never be another pastor like Ernest Laycock. He felt no one could combine the man's compassion with his ability to teach the Bible. Yet as Jerry quickly discovered, there is a wealth of talent on God's team.

"When Rev. Laycock stepped down," Jerry recalled, "Dr. Hubert Verrill was called to be the pastor at First Baptist Church. Dr. Verrill was educated at Denver Seminary. If I had any questions about him, they were answered the first time I heard him preach. He had the same kind of teaching style as did Rev. Laycock. When he preached he put the framework around the Scripture and then showed how it all related. He taught us that through history God had related to man in different ways. The more I heard him, the more the Bible made sense."

Jerry engaged the new preacher in conversations, and the men exchanged theological insights. Verrill even pulled books from his library to enhance Jerry's quest for biblical knowledge. As Jerry looked into this man's eyes, he saw the love and the faith God had in His children. Seeing that gave him a sense of awe he had never before experienced.

"Dr. Verrill saw my potential," Jerry explained. "He was my encourager. We would have fellowship, and he challenged me with new responsibilities. Then, when he developed cancer, he got me to preach when he was out. I could not believe he had that kind of confidence in me."

Seeing others respond to his words from the pulpit pushed Jerry into even deeper Bible study. As people were now looking to him for spiritual guidance, he naturally felt a responsibility few outside the ministry knew. So he constantly turned to the Bible to find the answers he needed for himself and others.

By now Jerry was no longer a grad student. He had given up on ecology and was now a high school teacher and a track and cross-country coach. He taught kids, prodding them to expand their minds while challenging their bodies. As he worked with his students on conditioning drills, as he pushed them to develop the self-discipline and self-motivation it took to win distance races, he realized that growing in the Lord required the same kind of effort and determination. Now Jerry was beginning to grasp a bigger picture too. It seemed that everything in his life was preparing him for something greater down the road. But for the moment he had no idea what that was.

Two other things had to fall into place for Jerry to understand his calling. The first came in the form of a failed seminary student named Jay Letty.

"Jay was my age," Jerry said. "He opened up a wealth of knowledge that I did not know existed. Because of his recent seminary studies, he was familiar with commentaries and study books written by spiritually solid men. This was thirty-five years ago, and I was not aware of the wealth of writers and teachers there were available to me through books. My wife and I spent a lot of time with Jay and his wife in the two years they lived here. Jay had such a passion for Christian growth. I could see it in his eyes, and his passion inspired me."

The more Jay and Jerry talked, the more they studied, the more Jerry treasured the Bible and the lessons found inside the book. He now saw God's Word as the greatest and most powerful tool in the world. With this concept entrenched in his mind and soul, the last piece of God's plan found its way to Jerry's doorstep.

Thanks to his speaking in church and his Sunday school classes, a local group saw Jerry's devotion to the Bible and faith in the Lord. These men approached Jerry and asked him to join them in the work of the Gideons. Jerry had heard of the organization and had seen their Bibles in motels, but he didn't have a clear understanding of how the group worked.

"As a teacher I was invited to become a member of the Gideons on a local level," Jerry recalled. "I discovered that it was an all-volunteer group, organized by state association. It had been founded in 1899 and was the oldest Christian business and professional men's association in the United States. And it was made up of laymen, just like me."

Jerry would also discover that the Gideons claimed more than a quarter of a million members living in 179 different countries, all united to accomplish the single objective of winning others to Christ. To meet this goal they were distributing tens of millions of Bibles annually. For a man who loved to study God's Word and felt that his growth in that Word was the most important thing in life, the Gideons offered Jerry a unique outlet. Therefore he didn't just join the group; he became their most enthusiastic member and hardest worker.

When Jerry spoke to churches and civic groups about the Gideons, he framed his remarks in scriptural lessons just as his three mentors had done. Because of his study, as well as his passion, Jerry grabbed audiences and plunged them into the Word. Those who heard him didn't just respond with support for placing Bibles in motels, hotels, hospitals, and other places; they opened their own Bibles and sought out meanings found in those pages for their own lives.

Over the years, Jerry rose through the ranks of Gideons International. He became one of their most requested speakers. Yet when the opportunity came to join the group full-time, he had to make a difficult choice.

"As a schoolteacher your life is pretty set," Jerry explained as he looked back on being asked to head up Gideons. "My wife and I were comfortable with our lives. If I took this position, then we would have to move to Nashville, and I would travel as many as four weeks at a time."

Yet for Jerry the answer to the call was obvious. This is where God wanted him. This is why three Spirit-filled men had come into his life and whetted his appetite for the Bible.

"I would not have the breadth of knowledge without those three men," Jerry readily admits. "The motivation they gave me is what prepared me. Now I not only get to study God's Word, but I get to see what that Word can do. When the Holy Spirit brings the understanding, it is so exciting."

Because of Laycock, Verrill, and Letty, Jerry felt a real need to grow in the Word. Thanks to them he understood the importance of knowing the Bible. And thanks to the men who reflected God and His passion in their words and eyes, Jerry is helping to take the Bible to millions each year. Much more than country music, it is Bibles that are Nashville's most powerful and most needed export, and you can see just how important they are when you look into Jerry Burden's eyes.

11

Hope Is Always Just around the Corner

James Scott Bell

Bestselling Christian Author

It was a bright sunny day with scarcely a cloud in the sky as the small boy and the elderly woman walked hand in hand down Hollywood Boulevard. The youngster's eyes darted from side to side as the two stepped across stars encrusted in the sidewalk marking the names of some of the world's greatest film, radio, and TV personalities. For the older woman it might have been a familiar scene, but for the child it was an incredible adventure. He was so caught up in the symbols of fame, he failed to notice the other side of the Hollywood experience.

In the shadows of the city's buildings, lingering like cheap perfume, were the wannabes who didn't find fame on celluloid, the tube, or the airwaves. These men and women were hopeless and hungry; their dreams had become nightmares that haunted them just as much in their waking hours as in their sleep. They were lurking on the fringes knowing they would never realize the bright spotlight of fame or fortune and were only concerned about their next meal or their next fix. They were for all practical purposes invisible to the boy and almost everyone who walked by. But not to the woman. She saw them. She had the courage to look into their faces, and when she did, some of the lost seemed to see something in Dot's eyes that gave them hope. They didn't know what she had that made her care for them, but they could sense her love. Though they probably didn't know it, as she walked on with her grandson, the silver-haired woman said a prayer for each of the city's forgotten souls.

After stepping over some of the most famous names on the globe and strolling by many of the best-known landmarks on the West Coast, this duo from different generations completed their trek at the Chinese Theater. The building's huge marquee trumpeted the latest biblical classic, *King of Kings*. As Dot bought the tickets, little Jim's eyes zeroed in on the footprints and handprints in the cement all around him. Clark Gable was there, as were John Wayne and Roy Rogers. Even at his young age, the child knew this would be a day he would always remember, and he was so grateful his grandmother had made it all possible. What he didn't know at that time was that it would be the blending of what he was to see that day with the images of what he failed to notice that would forever shape his life and put him on an avenue that would touch millions.

James Scott Bell is to modern Christian fiction what Raymond Chandler was to the crime readers of the 1930s and 1940s. Bell tells the tales of people immersed in darkness, caught on the wrong side of the law, men and women whose dreams have been dashed and who find hope as remote as the rings of Saturn. The author is so successful because he not only shows the world's seamy underbelly that results from falling to the lure of temptation but also builds a bridge to the world of forgiveness. To do this he sometimes shines a spotlight on the forgotten men and women his grandmother saw on the street that day. She prayed for them, and now he is telling their story and providing readers with the wisdom and salvation found in his grandmother's faith.

"When I was a kid," Jim recalls, "I used to love going into Hollywood and spending a few days at my grandparents' house. My grandmother, whom we all called 'Mama Dot,' used to take me to J. J. Newberrys and Grauman's Chinese Movie Theater. My grandparents had a house on Nichols Canyon Road, with a beautiful magnolia tree in the back yard. I'd sit out there in the summers and read or stare at the clouds, and eat Mama Dot's famous cheesecake."

What Bell had was a seemingly perfect grandmother. She would play with him, take him out to see the sights of the world, and make his favorite food. Yet if that was all she stood for, her influence would have faded with time, and she would not have so impacted his spiritual life. Yet this godly woman reflected Christ in spirit and touch. So when she hugged you, it was as if God Himself had thrown His arms around you. Jim felt that, and as he grew he began to see there was a great deal more to the woman than just the treats she offered on his visits.

"I heard stories from my dad how, during the Depression, guys would come by and she would feed them," Jim recounted.

As he began to understand what this action meant, her strong faith put into action began to mean more to the child than even her cheesecake. She looked beyond her own world and sought out those who needed to be lifted up to God. She cooked meals for countless men and women who didn't know her name. And she prayed that the kindness she had showed them would lead them to the Lord. Others would have run from the very people she sought out. That was the kind of courage she presented each day. It was courage that was completely grounded in faith.

Jim said, "One thing Mama Dot liked to say was, 'God and one is a majority.' She told me never to forget that, and I never have. That has always brought me comfort about my faith in times of need."

There was something about Dot that caused her grandson to stop and study her. She didn't possess movie-star looks or a vibrant personality. In fact, her quiet manner often caused her to blend into the background. Yet she used her soft manners to emphasize the essence of who she was.

"Mama Dot was always so gentle and loving and understanding. She was also the first person to tell me about God and the great Bible stories. I thrilled at the way she told them. She bought me a comic book about David and Goliath once, and I read it over and over. She also told me of the great victories of the Israelites. She told me those biblical tales right in her living room as I sat on what she always called 'the davenport.' At my feet was the handmade rug that she was always adding to. It got bigger every year."

Just as that rug grew larger and covered more and more of the living room, Mama Dot's impact on Jim grew as well. Rather than tell the same stories over and over again, she introduced him to different ones. The way she wove those moral tales was much like she made her cheesecake; the ingredients were the same as everyone else used, but the result was so much richer. Because Jim's parents did not attend church, Mama Dot's Bible stories were critical in preparing his heart to receive the Lord.

Dot may have paved the way, but he waited until he was a teenager to accept the Lord as his Savior. This was a move that his grandmother knew could not be forced and would have to come when he was ready. Bell was watching a Billy Graham crusade on television when he finally understood the salvation of which his grandmother had spoken so often. It was a revelation that moved him to his knees.

"When I accepted Christ an incredible feeling of warmth washed over me," Jim recalled. "For the first time I was connected to something higher than just this world."

That step in faith would begin a journey that took Bell to New York and back to Los Angeles, from Hollywood auditions to judges' chambers, from Shakespeare to Raymond Chandler and beyond. It would be a strange trip, maybe even more unbelievable than any adventures Bell would work into his bestselling novels, but the author had no doubt that God's hand was on him every stop along his way.

After high school Jim attended the University of California, Santa Barbara, where he played basketball, got a degree in film studies, and won a screenwriting award. He then moved on to New York to write for the theater. Even though he didn't claim to be an actor, he was first cast in a production of *Othello*, then in several off-Broadway productions, and finally in television commercials. As an actor Jim met his wife-to-be, an actress, and decided one thespian in the family was enough. The couple returned to Los Angeles, where Jim attended the University of Southern California law school, graduating with honors and winning the American Board of Trial Advocates' Award for Excellence. Then came a stint with one of L.A.'s top law firms before opening up his own office. Because of his brilliant legal work,

Bell was introduced to millions as a contributor to *Newsweek* and a commentator on *Good Morning America* and CBS radio.

Yet even with his fame now growing well beyond the courtroom, Jim was not satisfied. He yearned to be more creative and do it in a way that would feed the spirits of those who had never known faith. Perhaps it was the stories he heard from his grandmother, as well as all that Dot stood for, that drove him into fiction. His first novel, *The Darwin Conspiracy*, was a satirical romp through the early years of the evolutionary theory. He then moved into what would become his calling, penning legal thrillers. His first novel was *Circumstantial Evidence*, and several more have followed. *Final Witness* won the 2000 Christy Award as the top Christian suspense novel of the year. The author continued to grow as he teamed with Tracie Peterson to produce the bestselling Shannon Saga series. Then *Deadlock*, a tale about the U.S. Supreme Court, became a huge hit. By 2003 his success was so great that secular publishers requested he branch out and write the kind of potboilers that reach the top of the *New York Times* bestseller list. While he obviously has the talent to do just that, he had no desire to make the move away from Christian writing. Just as his grandmother always found a hungry person to feed during the Depression, Bell felt that many souls needed spiritual feeding in the twenty-first century.

Jim does not measure himself by the world's standards, but he does want to measure up to the standards he learned from his grandmother. That is why he has taught Sunday school for almost two decades and why he is constantly looking for ways to write new books that center on moral issues such as abortion, evolution, biotechnology, and faith under pressure. What really sets Bell's work apart is the fact that he builds a bridge that takes a person from darkness to light and from despair to hope.

"I guess I learned compassion from Mama Dot," Jim acknowledges. "She was so kind to people."

James Scott Bell first saw that Christian kindness in Mama Dot's eyes, and he felt it in her touch. Today millions see that same light in this writer's words. In this family faith has come full circle, and the blessings go on and on.

12

A Helping Hand at the End of a Long Walk

Denise Davis

Contemporary Christian Songwriter and Speaker

Denise Davis has a quiet, serene kind of beauty that belies the fact that she is a fighter, a dynamic and energetic go-getter. Though her deep blue eyes usually appear almost placid, this is a woman of action who not only performs contemporary Christian music but also composes songs that come from the depths of her soul. She is also a nationally recognized speaker, television host, and businesswoman. The fact Denise so deeply embraces life hides the fact she fights an unseen enemy. Like a menacing shadow on a stormy night, multiple sclerosis is always there, waiting, threatening, and demanding. For Denise this enemy is real, but it is never in control. With faith and determination that push her every move, this woman not only survives, she thrives! And a large part of this desire to battle on all fronts an unrelenting foe while always making a mighty difference for Christ can be traced back through the family tree to a Lawrenceburg, Tennessee, farm woman.

"When I was a little girl," Denise remembers, her blue eyes sparkling and a soft southern lilt wrapping around every word, "every summer I would go to my aunt Sarah Viola Mote's farm. Aunt Viola had three daughters and one son. For a city girl like myself from Russellville, Alabama, my annual trip to Lawrenceburg was a week filled with big adventures."

Each year, for a few hot humid summer days, Denise dismissed television, air-conditioning, and playing with her toys. While on her aunt Viola's farm, the wiry little girl with the long legs and the inexhaustible supply of energy was constantly on the move. It was almost as if she didn't feel the heat, driven on by an urge to keep up with a stocky, fair-skinned, redheaded woman whose work never seemed to be finished. Whether it was gathering eggs or weeding the vegetable garden, little Denise seemed to be in the way while always anxious to learn.

"How I remember the kindness in Aunt Viola's face," Denise explained. "I remember how patient she was with me. And when we finished a task, I remember how her hugs seemed to linger forever."

Besides doing the chores, raising her kids, and tending her beloved flower gardens, Viola was a driving force at her church. She was there every time the doors opened and made sure her kids, as well as any visitors at her home, such as Denise, were there as well. Her aunt's devotion to her church, as well as Viola's daily Bible reading and prayers, made a deep impression on Denise. She noted that no matter how busy her aunt was, she always found time for God and for teaching others about the Lord as well. Prayers with Aunt Viola were another special element of every day. So were the life lessons that seemed to be a part of every summer visit.

"When I was nine and having so much fun on the farm," Denise explained, "an uncle who lived down the road from Aunt Viola hitched up his horse to an old buggy and drove it to my aunt's. He offered to give us a ride back over to his place. I had never done anything like that before and really wanted to go, but my aunt had already told me a peddler was coming by her farm that afternoon. I didn't know what a peddler was, but when my aunt explained it to me, I got real excited. This man drove an old school bus filled with pots, pans, tools, books, dolls, pencils, and all kinds of other things I just had to see. So, being the stubborn little girl that I was, I was not going to get in that buggy until I was promised I would get back in time for the peddler's visit."

Denise was assured she would be back at her aunt's home before the peddler came. Yet exploring the new farm took much longer than anyone anticipated. And when she realized it was time for the peddler's visit and that her cousins didn't want to go home yet, the city girl panicked. She called her aunt.

"I demanded to be taken back right then," Denise recalled. "When I was told it wasn't time yet and if I would just wait a little while and then we would ride back over to my aunt's, I got mad and struck out walking. I had to see the peddler and his bus and nothing was going to stop me. I had no shoes on and the gravel road made it feel like this tenderfooted city girl was walking on nails. I would take a few steps, cry a little, then take a few more steps. Yet as bad as it hurt, I was not going to turn back.

"My uncle called Aunt Viola and told her what was going on. She must have considered the situation for a few seconds before deciding to teach me a lesson. She didn't want to reward my impatience, so she didn't immediately come to get me. I hobbled on for more than a mile, then pretty much gave up. By this time I knew I couldn't make it on my own."

Sobbing along the side of the road, Denise felt more alone than she had ever felt in her life. She knew there was no way she could finish the trip by herself. Then, through tear-filled eyes, she looked up and saw her aunt strolling down the road to meet her. They stood looking at each other for a few moments, then together, hand in hand, they walked back to the farm, Denise still barefoot.

"I missed the peddler," Denise admitted, "and I could see that my aunt was not happy with me. Worse yet, for the next few days every time I took a step on my bruised, cut feet, I realized that being stubborn could be terribly painful."

As the years flew by, times with Aunt Viola took on a new meaning. Denise learned that this woman who had not bowed to Denise's demands to be immediately picked up would sacrifice everything to be there for the most important moments in her niece's life.

"I know that I was a pain from time to time," Denise explained, "but my aunt Viola and her daughters loved me unconditionally. They always made the long trips to be there when I graduated from high school or when I performed in church or at a local event. As my awards and honors mounted up, there was no jealousy and no backbiting, just happiness, pride, and support."

Aunt Viola's pride mounted, when, as a teen, Denise recorded her first records at the famed Muscle Shoals (an Alabama studio), was crowned the youngest ever Miss Alabama, performed in a USO tour of Asia, and accepted a scholarship to the University of Alabama at Florence. Aunt Viola was there when, after college,

Denise began to open for Lee Greenwood, George Jones, and the Gatlin Brothers. The older woman proudly told her friends about her niece's recording soundtracks for the daytime dramas *Santa Barbara* and *Sunset Beach*. A few years later it was Viola who first showed off Denise's modeling ads for the Castner Knott department store, Drexel Heritage Furniture, and Maybelline.

Achieving goals seemed to be easy for Denise. Her potential to achieve anything she wanted appeared to be endless. Then, just when she was ready to make the next big move in Music City, the energetic young woman began to tire easily. Within weeks her legs grew numb. One night, while playing piano, her world suddenly went dark. With no warning, she found herself blind.

It took several weeks and scores of tests for a neurologist to diagnose that multiple sclerosis was rampaging through Denise's body, but it took only a few hours for Viola to assure her niece that everything would be fine. The farm woman calmly told Denise this might be a rocky path, but she could make it. And that if she needed help, the stocky woman with the red hair would be there each step of the way.

As Denise fought to escape a dark world, Viola fell to her knees and asked God for a miracle. As she prayed, Viola had faith not just in the Lord's power but also in her niece's strength and determination. She knew that Denise now needed that strong will that had been exhibited on the rocky walk so many years before.

In the hospital, night after night, Denise stubbornly tried to battle her problems on her own. With an independent streak a mile wide, she told everyone she could make this trip by herself. She didn't need any help. But the dawn didn't break, her world continued to be immersed in darkness, and the young woman could not even find the beginning of the path to the next phase of her life. Finally, her will broken, Denise admitted to the Lord she couldn't do it by herself. When she acknowledged her own impatience and weakness, a sense of power filled her. It was as if a strong hand was there leading her down a much smoother road.

Several months later Denise's sight returned, along with a desire to perform only Christian music from then on. Johnny Rutenschroer signed her as a writer for Life Music Group. Within a few months Denise was back in the studio to record an album. *Eternally Grateful*, her first inspirational project, garnered five chart singles and launched a career that found Denise constantly in demand in churches and women's conferences. And whenever she could, Aunt Viola, her blue eyes misting, would proudly watch her niece touch others for Christ. With a strength that even surprised her, Denise again felt she could handle anything the world tossed her way. Then, as often happens, life threw her another curveball.

"One of the darkest days of my life came when my mother called me and told me Aunt Viola had cancer," Denise recalled. "It was the first Sunday in May when she came to Vanderbilt for tests. I called her and she told me there was no hope, that she was a goner, and they were sending her home to die. I immediately went to the hospital to see her. As I walked up to the door, I thought I was going to fall apart. Yet I entered the room and I found Aunt Viola and her daughters laughing and cutting up. It was as if nothing was wrong. I couldn't figure out what was going on. As I looked into my aunt's penetrating blue eyes — eyes that even now seemed so happy, youthful, peaceful — I was so troubled and confused. I simply could not understand how my aunt could feel such peace at this horrible moment in her life."

Denise wanted to run. She didn't want to face her dying aunt or try to come up with the words she felt she needed to say. Rather than continue to struggle to keep her composure, Denise turned and stared blankly out the window.

"Aunt Viola grabbed my hand," Denise explained. "As I looked into her eyes, I suddenly felt as if I was looking at the eyes of God. I had never seen such peace, such joy. She knew she was dying. Yet she wasn't concerned. She knew the moment death came she would immediately be meeting Jesus Christ. She was cool with it."

Somehow sensing Denise's confusion, the older woman smiled and said, "I'm fine with this, but I will miss you, child. I love you, you know!"

The younger woman struggled for something to say before finally sobbing, "Tell Jesus I hope He likes my music."

"I will," Viola replied. "And Denise, I'm sorry I made you walk all the way home that day."

Denise looked up then, and as if a light had suddenly illuminated the darkness and doubt, she smiled. Her spiritual blindness had been removed, and she too felt the joy of a woman who knew the road home would be easy if she just waited on the Lord to walk with her along the way. Viola Mote didn't have to wait long; a week later she died at home on the farm she loved.

Denise's cousins still rib her about the long walk on the gravel road. Yet the lesson she learned that day has made her eternally grateful her aunt did not drop everything and come to grant her selfish wishes. That long walk set in motion a course of events that allowed Denise to humble herself before her Lord, accept His help, and live a life that continues to inspire thousands each year. This aunt who loved unconditionally taught a young girl how to walk with the Lord.

13

The Power of a Single Prayer

Fern Nichols

Author and Leader of Moms In Touch International

An old saying goes, "There is no one in heaven who hasn't been prayed for." Fern Nichols both believes this phrase and lives it every day. The organization she founded two decades ago, Moms In Touch International, claims more than 150,000 prayer partners in nations all around the globe. United by the belief that prayer is the first step in releasing the power, protection, and grace found through Jesus Christ, mothers the world over are dramatically impacting the daily lives of children everywhere through prayer. Yet this movement, begun by an individual woman in Canada, would have never sent forth a single prayer if it had not been for a twenty-two-year-old mother of four tuning in to an Oregon radio station half a century ago.

"My mother grew up poor," Fern explained. "She was just an ordinary girl before she got married. She was not well educated and had little direction. By God's hand, she met my dad at a dance. He had lost his wife when his second child was born.

He swept Mom off her feet, and they got married. Though she was just nineteen, she was instantly a mother to a six-year-old and a baby. Seventeen months later I was born, and then less than two years later my sister came along."

With so much to do each day, Marie never thought about going to church or saying a prayer. God was a far-off element that was a part of a distant universe, so He didn't enter her mind much either. Yet in her demanding daily grind she did come to feel that something was missing in her life. She couldn't explain it to her husband or friends, but an emptiness haunted her crowded world day in and day out.

For many mothers of the post–World War II era, the radio offered companionship. Over the airwaves came familiar voices who almost became some of Marie's dearest friends. One of those voices spoke daily of the power of having Christ as one's Savior. Marie began to listen to that voice more and more, and as she did, she also began to question if Jesus might just be able to fill the void in her heart and life.

"Every day she would listen to Christian radio," Fern remembered, "and on one 'God' day, she gave her life to the Lord. And truly from that day on it was like a 180-degree turnaround. There is a verse in Joshua that says, 'For me and my house we will serve the Lord.' From the moment she accepted Christ that was truly what Mom was very intentionally trying to do."

As a new Christian, the first thing Marie felt she needed was a church. Since she wasn't raised in a family that went to church, she wasn't real sure how to go about finding one. She decided the easiest thing to do was simply attend the house of worship nearest to her front door. A mile down the road was St. John's Baptist. On the first Sunday morning after she was saved, Marie bundled up her kids and headed toward that little building. Though she couldn't explain why, she felt as if she was coming home for the very first time.

As Marie and her four kids walked in, a small woman with a big smile was there to greet them. Mrs. Pomroy would become more than a welcoming voice; she would soon step into the roles of both grandmother and mentor to Marie and her children. The fact that Mrs. Pomroy was active in every facet of the church made a big impact on Marie. Without even realizing it, the young mother began to be affected by this outgoing bundle of energy.

There are many young mothers who join churches to get a chance to take a break from their kids. Few could have faulted Marie if this was what she had done. Some of the members might have been guilty of thinking, "Well, she just wants to dump the children in our laps and sleep late one morning a week." But as they would soon find out, Marie was ready to have her faith make an impact.

"So it was not that she got saved and just sent us to church," Fern remembered, "but she went with us and served. I think this is why I love the body of Christ so much today; I saw her joy in serving. She was superintendent of the beginners, she would roll bandages for mission work, she was in charge of a girls' group called King's Daughters. If there was a need, she was there to meet it. The church became our second family. She actually lived out the admonition of Deuteronomy 6."

Church was the beginning but not the end of the young mother's giving her life to the Lord's work. Overcome with the presence of God in her life, she began Bible devotions with her children, developed daily family prayers before meals and at bedtime, and often stopped on a moment's notice to offer special prayers.

"She impressed on us children," her daughter recalls, "that when we sat up, when we sat down, when we went along the way, we should pray. We had devotions at night, and there was not a meal that we didn't pray and give God thanks for our food. Oftentimes before we left the driveway in the car to go to school, church, or anywhere else, she would pray for our protection."

In her mother Fern saw a woman of prayer. On a moment's notice Marie would close her eyes, bow her head, and offer thanks, praise, or a need to God. Praying soon became as natural as breathing to the beautiful young woman. Yet prayer was just the beginning; she was also constantly looking for ways to put her faith into action.

"My mom's faith was an alive faith. I saw in her beautiful blue eyes a determination to serve the Lord—a determination of faith. She probably wouldn't have put it in those words. In her mind she just responded each moment to how the Holy Spirit was leading her. As she was very new in her faith, she was kind of growing in her faith as she was growing with us. As I think back, I realized that the Lord takes an ordinary little person and puts a supernatural God inside them. That was what was happening to my mom. She was just being faithful in the ordinary, mundane things, but when that faith was touched with the supernatural, it became a place where God's glory dwells and is seen. That sums up her life—she was faithful in the ordinary things, and those produced mighty results." It would be another generation before the sum of those mighty results became obvious.

Marie's spiritual beauty was almost rivaled by her physical appearance. She not only was born with beauty but was very disciplined about always looking her best. This was just a facet of her personality that carried over to everything she did. She kept a spotless house, her kids were always neat, and her spiritual life was just as well ordered. Part of her discipline was being prepared when she taught a Sunday school lesson or worked with a children's choir.

"I began playing piano for her Sunday school classes when I was nine." Fern laughed as she recalled the experience. "She would look at me with those eyes to see if I was ready. She would also let me know that when I was playing in God's service, then I had better be totally prepared. I was to always give my best for Him."

In the days of working with her mother at church, Fern learned something else that would become instrumental in her own life. Marie saw herself as part of God's team. Therefore she worked hard to be ready to do her part. She knew that if she was not prepared, if she did not give it everything she had, then the team would not measure up either. This discipline and sense of teamwork were passed along to her children. They each learned they were a part of God's team and were expected to give Him everything they had. All they had to do to realize the full importance of their work was to look at the faith and determination in their mother's eyes.

"When you are growing up you don't always see the love of Jesus in those eyes," Fern explained. "Sometimes you see correction, but that really is the love of Christ. What she was instilling in us was discipline in life. To this day there is discipline in my life, prayer time, and quiet time — the things she passed along to me. Because of what she taught me, I was purposeful in not missing church. I served in the church and was very active in the church with my kids. And like my mother, it was not out of the law, but it was out of the extreme gratefulness and love we had for the Lord."

Though she would be a part of every youth activity in her church, it would be as a mother that she fully appreciated her mother's faith and what it could mean in a dark and dangerous world. While living in Canada, Fern suddenly grew very apprehensive about sending her boys to junior high.

"I had heard about the bad things that were happening in our school," Fern recalled, "and I felt a need to pray for protection for my children."

The young mother suddenly remembered back to her childhood and Wednesday prayer meetings. Each week she was there with her mother in the pews as the congregation of St. John's Baptist Church came together to share praises and pray for special needs. Fern remembered how secure she felt when she left those meetings, how strong even a child's faith was when it was immersed in the prayers of fellow believers.

"I decided that I needed someone to pray with me for our school and our children. I called a friend, and she was willing to join me for one hour a week dedicated to prayer."

What sprang from this first prayer meeting was a movement. Initially the group was small, but as others found out about the prayer meetings, more and more came. And the praying didn't stop when the group said their final "amen." Like Marie had done when raising her kids, the members of the group found themselves praying for the school's children all the time. For most, prayer became as natural as breathing.

"When I first formed the prayer group," Fern explained, "I wanted it to be intentional, I wanted it to be disciplined, I wanted it to be on a regular basis, and I wanted us to give our emotions and concerns to the One who could do something about them. Together, with just a few other moms, it was a truly humble beginning."

When her husband was transferred to California, Fern wondered if she could start a new prayer group there. God sent the first mother of this group right up to her front door, and the prayer ministry grew from there. Soon scores were coming together to pray for the kids at this school too. When word got out, others in nearby districts began asking how they could start a group of praying mothers in their communities as well.

"These women discovered that prayers make a difference," Fern explained. "In Ezekiel 22:30, it points out that if just one person had stood in the gap, Israel would not have been destroyed. Just like I had learned from my mother, I shared with these other mothers the power of one life, the value of one life, and that just being obedient to the Lord where He has you will create a rippling effect beyond what we can see and know."

Over just a few years the Moms In Touch group grew from a single group to thousands all across the globe. Using Fern's book *Every Child Needs a Praying Mom* as a guide, mothers in more than fifty different countries began coming together weekly to pray for their children and their schools. The difference in their kids and their schools soon became obvious. There was light where there had once been darkness; there was purpose where there had once been emptiness. The differences were as defined as had been the difference in Marie the day she was saved through the message of a voice on the radio.

"I never lived an unredeemed life like my mom did," Fern recalled, "because I was brought up in the faith and accepted Christ at a very young age. I learned as a child that Mom was serving not because she had to but because she wanted to. I could see that desire in her eyes and hear it in her prayers. I saw the difference it made in our lives too.

"Long after we are dead the legacy of our prayers will continually be played out in the things to come. Mom knew that, and I am so thankful that in her life she shared that with me."

Moms In Touch International was started and is guided by a dynamic woman named Fern Nichols. Yet if it weren't for the devotion and example of a woman named Marie, perhaps this organization might not have existed. Because of Marie, thousands of prayers have been offered for children, and millions of lives have been touched. That is the power of one mother's life and prayers, the power that could be seen in her actions and in her eyes.

14

You Can Go Home Again

Larry Gatlin

Grammy Award – Winning
Singer and Songwriter

On a muggy summer Sunday night a lively throng had gathered outside the Oak Cliff Assembly of God Church. In spite of the heat, these families had put aside a host of other interests and activities, left their modest homes, loaded into well-worn cars, and come together to worship the Lord. With Bibles in hand, they had initially lingered outside in the parking lot, seeking the minimal relief of a faint breeze while sharing stories of baseball, fishing, relations, and local news. They talked about the upcoming election, and whether the handsome Democrat from Massachusetts could beat the vice president. Then, as the sun began to sink and the sounds of a piano called them inside, the conversations subsided and the people moved toward the front steps.

As they had a hundred times before, one by one the church members entered the large wooden doors and found their places. Settling into familiar pews, each one eagerly anticipated the coming time of praise and worship. On this hot night, women and children pulled from the racks in front of them fans donated by a local funeral parlor and gently stirred the thick air. The men ignored the fans, preferring to roll up the sleeves of their starched white shirts and loosen their thin ties. As they readied their bodies for a futile fight against the muggy heat, they prepared their souls to receive something much more refreshing than any cool breeze.

As the worship hour drew near, they began to look up toward the pulpit. As they did, they were greeted by the large smile and warm eyes of their pastor, the Reverend H. C. Noah. Brother Noah was a beloved man, a preacher who treated his flock as if they were his own children. To these people, his words had meaning and impact, and when he spoke of glory, they believed. Yet, unknown to the members, this night was going to be special. On this Sunday evening their hearts would be stirred not only by the pastor's message but by the music of a quartet from faraway Odessa, Texas.

After a few congregational songs and a call to prayer, Brother Noah introduced the four children and their mother. Taking a deep breath, twelve-year-old Larry Gatlin, followed by his younger brothers Steve and Rudy and his sister LaDonna, walked up to the front of the sanctuary. The boys were dressed in their best clothes, their hair was perfectly groomed and kept in place with a generous supply of tonic, and the room's yellow lights caught the shine of their black shoes. LaDonna smoothed out the ruffled skirt of her dress as they took places at the front of the church. As kids go, they were immaculate. Throughout the room, mothers were elbowing their own sons and daughters to take note.

In unison the quartet took a deep breath and waited for their mother's cue from the piano. As they began to sing a medley of hymns taken from the tattered pages of an old Stamps-Baxter songbook, the Spirit of the Lord seemed to break through the night's repressive heat like a breath of fresh air. Within seconds every eye was glued to the Gatlin Quartet. The congregation hung on each note, listened to each word, and when the foursome finished, a chorus of "Amens" and "Hallelujahs" echoed from wall to wall.

Smiling, the beloved preacher rose from his chair and spoke of the joy of music mixed with the enthusiasm of youth. And on that hot Texas night, through these four children, the Lord's cool, life-giving Spirit came down and touched the congregation. They knew they had been blessed by a great message in song, yet they couldn't have realized that what they had just witnessed was a mere preview of the deep potential and influence of these uniquely talented siblings.

On that night, as a fresh-faced Larry Gatlin sat beside his mother on a hard wooden pew, he also didn't know that the words of a preacher were going to profoundly affect him not just at this moment but forever. Raised in a Christian family, surrounded by solid values, Larry was a model child. Yet even as his family had helped prepare a foundation of faith, the real work on building the walls of that faith probably began on this night.

"As a kid," Larry Gatlin recalled, his expressive eyes focusing on things in his distant past, "we used to drive from Odessa and go to this church in Oak Cliff to sing. My mother played the piano. While we were there I heard Brother H. C. Noah — isn't that a great name for a preacher? — preach incredible sermons. His words were so anointed of God they made me, even at a young age, want to believe and try his way. When he preached about Christ and the love of God, a light showed in his face that made me believe what he preached about was real. It wasn't some fairy story or some comic book deal."

Even back home in West Texas, the young boy would from time to time chew on the preacher's words, remembering the way the message had made him feel. And every time he and his brothers made that long drive to Brother Noah's church, he felt a special joy simply from walking into the building.

Time passed, the boys grew, and the trips to Oak Cliff were often replaced with football games, high school dances, and dating. Yet even though the trips were fewer, the young man still thought often about Brother Noah.

After high school Larry registered at the University of Houston. Among other things, he found a place on the football team. When he discovered his athletic scholarship didn't foot the entire bill for his education, he was forced to find a part-time job. The eager freshman with the quick wit and instant smile applied for a position as the janitor at the Calvary Assembly of God Church in Pasadena, Texas. It paid ten dollars a month. With the Lord's influence all around him, Larry was in good hands, and his life was filled with the impact of good people.

"I was very privileged to sit under the preaching of a wonderful old-time preacher, Rev. Joe Neely," Larry explained. "Joe Neely was a very special man. One morning he was there while I was cleaning up his office, and he saw an article that said A. A. Alan, a noted evangelist, had died. Well, Brother Neely saw this article and stuck his head down on his desk and began crying softly.

"I said, 'What's wrong, Preacher?' And he said, 'Asa's dead!'

"I looked over his shoulder, read the article, and asked, 'You mean you knew A. A. Alan?' This man was a really famous evangelist from the thirties. Then he told me, 'Larry, back in the twenties and thirties, A. A. Alan and I started over a hundred churches by ourselves up in the mining camps in Colorado and Wyoming.' He proceeded to tell me that they'd pack into these mining camps back in Colorado, Wyoming, and Utah on horseback with mules carrying their equipment. They'd tie their mules to the hitching post, get a Bible, and walk up in the middle of the street in the mud, in the blood and the beer, or whatever was there, and they'd open the Bible and begin preaching the truth of Jesus Christ. He sat there for an hour and told me stories of those experiences, and it impacted me deeply."

For four years Houston offered Larry Gatlin a place to grow and find himself. It also reinforced his belief that he wanted to pursue a career in music, despite the overwhelming odds against this small-town boy. Armed with a guitar, a headstrong faith, and a stubborn will, he tried to interest the world in his songs. Hard work and persistence paid off, and by the early seventies he earned recognition when Elvis Presley recorded one of his gospel efforts, "Help Me," and another of his country numbers, "The Bigger They Are, the Harder They Fall." For the young songwriter these two compositions would be both the beginning of a wildly successful career and the foretaste of things to come.

To make his mark as an entertainer, Larry returned home and picked up the other members of his childhood family trio. The Gatlins then became country music's best vocal trio for more than a decade. They won Grammy Awards, performed before packed houses around the world, appeared countless times on national television, sold millions of records, and earned more money than anyone in Oak Cliff, Texas, had ever seen. With a beautiful wife and family, the respect of the music industry, and the adoration of millions of fans, Larry should have been happy. But beneath the mask of success, demons were pulling at him, slowly eating away at the very fiber of his being.

Like so many of his generation, Larry Gatlin fell under the spell of cocaine and alcohol. For years no one knew, and he vigorously denied that these addictive substances had any control over him. Like millions of others, he found it easy to rationalize his use of drugs. But although the world was fooled, he discovered he couldn't fool himself. The joy that once filled the young boy who had sung in Oak Cliff, the zest for life that fueled the college student, the freshness and vigor that inspired the young songwriter, were now slipping away. He was plunging deeper and deeper into a hole that seemed to have neither a bottom nor a way out. Walls were closing in, the clock was ticking, and new fears seemed to be around every corner. Then, after two straight days of doing drugs and alcohol, when things were at their darkest, when he was feeling more lost than he had ever felt, when he had no hope left, Larry sought out an old friend.

That evening, while staying at a hotel in Phoenix, Arizona, Larry found himself in the middle of his worst drug binge ever. As high as a kite and yet lower than he had ever been before, he decided to take drastic action. Panicked, paranoid, and alone, he struggled to the phone and began a search for Joe Neely. On his first call, he discovered the preacher no longer lived in Houston. For hours, he faced nothing but closed doors, but Larry finally tracked Neely to Temple, Texas. With his heart in his throat, Larry dialed the number. There was no answer. Needing to see God in the face of this old friend caused the singer to take drastic action.

Practically crawling into the airport, Larry caught a plane to Texas, rented a car, and somehow found his way to Temple. There, he was given directions to Joe Neely's rural church. Driving as fast as he could, he skidded to a stop in front of the modest building and raced to the front doors. Catching his breath, he said a short prayer, and then walked in. The former church janitor was now thirty-four years old. He was looking for answers, direction, hope, and after a mad day and night of frantic travel, he had come to a place where he thought he might be able to find them.

"In the midst of terrible drug addiction and confusion and alcoholism," Larry recalled, "I went to see Joe Neely. I hadn't seen him in thirteen years. As I walked into the church, he was giving a little talk on his recent missionary visits to Greece and Italy."

When Larry entered, the two men's eyes met. Immediately the preacher sensed the visitor's pain. Holding up his hand, he quit talking for a moment and then smiled. In a voice filled with joy and grace he said, "Folks, there's a young man right here who's been like a son to me, and I haven't seen him in thirteen years. I've got to hug him right now." Larry Gatlin stood perfectly still as he once again looked into the eyes of his old friend. He felt both exhilaration and embarrassment. He was humbled beyond words, and yet he knew that for the first time in years, he was home.

"I ran down that aisle" — Larry smiled as he spoke of that time — "and we hugged. I felt loved and accepted. I stayed in Temple for a while, and over the next two or three days Joe and

I visited a great deal. During this time he was very instrumental in making me know that no matter what—despite what I had done, despite how low I had sunk, despite the fact that I was into drugs, alcohol, and gambling, that I had acted crazy, that I was turning away from God—he loved me.

"I'll never forget what he told me. 'Larry,' he said, 'I don't care what you've done, I still love you. And just think how much more capacity God has to love you than I do!' Boy, did that hit me. His words really hit home, and I've never forgotten them. He's been a dear friend ever since."

Joe Neely's words, compassion, and gaze reflected the love and acceptance of Jesus Christ. This was what Gatlin needed to take a first step back to a God-centered life. But the visit, and what he felt and said there, only initiated the turnaround. The weight of getting back on the right track fell on Larry's own shoulders. He had to admit to himself, to the world, and to God that he had a problem. Two years after racing down the aisle to meet his old pastor, after countless ups and downs, Larry finally realized he needed real help. He simply couldn't do it by himself.

Swallowing what was left of his pride, he checked into the medical facility of the Orange County Care Unit. There he realized just how difficult it was going to be to get all the way back. Drugs, alcohol, and gambling had reduced Larry to a man on his knees begging the Lord to "help me." And that help arrived just when he needed it most.

"Dr. Joe Pursch," Larry recalled, "who was the director of the medical facility where I went for treatment for my drug and alcohol problem, called me on the phone and said, 'You need to meet a man named Jack Boland.' Unbeknownst to Joe Pursch, I was listening to some of Jack's tapes at that time. A cold chill ran down my spine. Well, actually it wasn't a cold chill, it was more like warm oil on top of my head, and Joe arranged the meeting.

"Jack Boland had been a hopeless alcoholic, and at twenty-nine he thought his life was over. He then came into a fellowship called Alcoholics Anonymous and was sober for the rest of his life. He wound up being the pastor of the Church of Today, a large Unity Church in Detroit, Michigan."

Larry found Jack to be unlike any preacher he had ever met. Having been in the gutter himself, Jack was aware of the pain and suffering that are a part of every addict's life. And having found the Lord, he also understood the richness of a full spiritual life. His faith was uncomplicated. When he spoke, the gospel had never seemed so simple.

"His Christian faith and his belief were a little bit different from Joe Neely's and Brother Noah's," Larry explained. "He took the Sermon on the Mount and the things that Christ said to do and he said, 'Do those things. Forget about all the other demagoguery, and the lighting of the candles, and the trappings of religion. Do what the Master Teacher said to do, and your life will be full. Therein is salvation.'

"He told me to love my neighbor as myself and that others will know that we are His disciples if we love one another. It looks to me that in a lot of churches we don't even love the ones sitting next to us, much less the people on the other side of town who go to a different church. Jack Boland brought this into focus for me. It suddenly became apparent that if you simply take the Beatitudes that Jesus taught in the fourth, fifth, and sixth chapters of Matthew and live those, then you will find the salvation of the world."

Every day is a challenge to someone with an addiction, but it is a challenge that Larry Gatlin is more than willing to face. Through the inspiration of three very different men, he has been grounded and regrounded in the knowledge of what makes life worth living. Larry also knows that no matter what he does, he can't repay these men for what they have taught him. In these three he saw Jesus, and for each man that would be thanks enough.

"On the day Jack Boland died," Larry related, "he called and asked me to sing 'Amazing Grace' to him over the phone. When I finished he said, 'Larry, tell your brothers I said hello, not goodbye.' He went on to the other side with a smile on his face.

"In the years I knew him, the many days we talked, I never heard him say a bad thing about a single human being. I never saw him, even in the throes of cancer, without a smile on his face. He proved to me that all I need to do is to go to the Bible and take the part that's written in red. And I try to do that. I just take the red part and try to live by that. Jack Boland taught me that, and he was a man who lived it every day of his life."

In the fall of 1991, long after summer's heat had been beaten away, Larry, Steve, and Rudy Gatlin drove back to a small church outside of Dallas, Texas. One of the church's most revered members was having his eighty-sixth birthday, and they had come to sing for him. As they walked in, the Reverend H. C. Noah, his voice still strong and his mind still sharp, was teaching a Sunday school lesson on Noah's ark. Larry looked into the man's eyes and saw that same fire he had first recognized more than thirty years before. *Jesus is there in those eyes*, he thought. Later, as Larry and his brothers stepped to the front of the church, time faded away for both the preacher and the singer, and the innocence of another moment was realized again.

No one can make a moment last forever. When the time is over, we must move on. Yet in leaving Brother Noah's small church that day, Larry Gatlin realized something vitally important. When it comes to the Lord and His family, you can always go home again.

Gatlin still sings and performs today, not only in country music, but also dropping in from time to time to join Bill Gaither at his Homecoming concerts. Here, once again, Larry sings the music of his youth with the spirit and convictions of someone who has been saved by grace. With the help of three powerful men — H. C. Noah, Joe Neely, and Jack Boland — Larry Gatlin found that the Lord's arms are always open wide to take him back, no matter what.

15

A Blind Date with God

Richard Stearns
Head of World Vision

The irony of first seeing Jesus in another's eyes on a blind date is never lost on Richard Stearns. He knows that without that chance meeting, he would probably not now be a Christian, much less be leading the massive missions of World Vision. So what happened that night during his senior year of college had to be part of a divine plan. Nothing else could explain the change that began then and continues to this day to impact Rich and millions of the world's "least of these."

"I was a senior at Cornell," Rich explained, looking back three decades, "and I wasn't a believer. I went out on a blind date with Reneé. Her roommate fixed us up. She described Reneé as being a goody-two-shoes Jesus freak who needed a dose of reality. Her roommate thought I would be good for her.

"It was about a month before I graduated, so I had nothing to lose. Besides, Reneé was pretty, a California blond with a beautiful smile. As the evening continued I discovered a dignity in the way she carried herself, and I could tell she had real character. She had ideals and was a presidential scholar. She was the type of girl you brought home to meet Mom and Dad. She was a breath of fresh air compared with the other girls I usually dated who hung out at the bars.

"We went to a movie and a coffeehouse. As we sat there chatting she took a tract on the four spiritual laws from her purse. She then said, 'God loves you, and He has a plan for your life.'

"I remember thinking, *Are you kidding?*"

Rich left the Catholic church when he was a kid. He came from a broken home, where he had experienced the devastation of being the child of an alcoholic. He believed that Christianity and the Bible were nothing but adult fairy tales. A neurobiology major, he saw life in its most logical form. If it could not be measured in a lab, it was not real. So Reneé could hand out tracts and talk about God all she wanted, but he was not going to buy into it. Yet because she was so beautiful he let the young woman ramble for a little while, then changed the subject.

"I asked her what she was studying," he recalled. "She told me that she had known since she was a kid that she was going to major in government, go to law school, and then help the poor in the inner cities. I thought her goal was a noble thing. I then informed her that I was going to get an MBA from Wharton, be a CEO, and make a lot of money."

Even though he didn't take anything the innocent young coed said seriously, he was fascinated by her. Though he thought she was a bit naive about the real world, he was intrigued by her sincerity. So he opted to build on what had become a very strange first date. He figured that given time she would come around to his way of thinking.

"She was unlike anyone I had ever dated," Rich recalled. "She was nice, sincere, and sweet. Over the next few weeks, I ran into her on campus, we shared more cups of coffee, we studied together, and she invited me to her pledge formal."

Though Rich couldn't put his finger on it, something about Reneé continued to pull him toward her. Logically this pull made no sense. He was about to leave Cornell and knew he could offer no future to this freshman, yet it was as if he couldn't help himself. He even put up with the theological debates just to be with her. For a young man who had always been an avid member of the school's party scene, this type of innocent dating was like nothing he had ever experienced. It was like being hooked on a drug. Reneé seemed to have something that he needed.

"As things started to get more serious," Rich remembered, "the difference in our religious worldviews became more of a problem. We got to a point where we argued when we discussed religion. I was so logical and stubborn, and she related only to things that came from her heart. At times these discussion ended with angry words and tears. She went back home to California at the end of the semester, and I went to upstate New York."

Rich and Reneé spent the summer getting to know each other through letters. In writing, their arguments were far less heated. Though they could come to no agreement on her faith and his lack of it, their time apart caused them to count the days until they could see each other again. When the summer finally ended and their fall terms started, Rich found reasons to make the trip from Wharton to Cornell. He simply couldn't wait to see Reneé again.

"In the fall," he recalled, "I would make that five-hour drive once or twice each month. Though I couldn't wait to see her when I left, the Christian faith thing caused arguments, and our visits didn't always go well. Finally, after another night of debating our faith, I informed her I was never going to believe what she believed. For me to change would take a 'walking on water miracle.' I then added, 'You have a choice to make, and we aren't going to talk about this again. It is going to be either me or God.'"

As she studied the man she loved, a fire burned in Reneé's eyes. Rich could see that glow as well. And because of that look, he sensed the end of their relationship was at hand. Standing as tall as she could, she boldly stated, "You have given me no choice. I could never marry someone who doesn't share my faith. I guess it's over."

"I often think of the courage she had that night," Rich pointed out. "We really loved each other. But on that day she told me whom she would serve, and she chose the Lord."

The two didn't see each other for several months. When the Christmas school break came, Reneé went back to California, and Rich went back to New York, bored beyond reason.

"It was January, I had nothing to do, and none of my bar-hopping buddies were around. I began looking through boxes of some of my old stuff and found a book called *Basic Christianity* by John Stott. A high school girlfriend had given me the book years before. I started reading it. Once I got started, I couldn't stop. When I finished the book at four in the morning, I was trembling. The Holy Spirit was working on me. The next day I went to a bookstore and bought a dozen heavy books on religion. I read for a week and then called Reneé."

Reneé was shocked to hear from Rich. She was even more stunned that he was excited about studying the Bible. When he asked for her advice on what to read in the Bible, she told him to start with John and see where it led.

"Once I got started, I couldn't stop reading. I was being drawn closer and closer. I was like a lawyer in court, looking at faith on the weight of the evidence. Finally, after several months of reading, I realized that if I had to choose, I now believed that it was most likely true. At that moment I got on my knees right in my dorm at Wharton, gave my life to God, and asked Him for His help."

Rich was at first surprised that he didn't feel any different. But once he made the step in faith, he began to understand that he *was* different. He looked outward rather than inward. He noticed the emptiness in others and wondered how he ever found any kind of satisfaction in his old life. He may have felt the same, but his vision was much different.

"I called Reneé," Rich explained, "and I asked her what it all meant. When she got back to school we started seeing each other again, and I found out she had been praying for me. As I grew in my faith, we started to go to church. In June of 1975 we were married."

Right after they said their "I dos," Rich and Reneé began to live the dreams they had shared with each other on the night they met. He became a businessman, an intelligent dynamo who worked his way up various corporate ladders and was quickly recognized as a star in his field. Reneé went to law school and fulfilled her goal of helping the poor through a job in legal services. She left her calling only when the family grew to the point where the Stearns' children (they have five) needed Reneé more as a mom than social services needed her as an attorney. And even without her paycheck, everything the couple touched still seemed to turn to gold.

After two decades of marriage, Rich and Reneé found themselves living in a two-hundred-year-old, ten-bedroom house on a five-acre estate in Pennsylvania. He was the CEO of Lenox, one of the world's top luxury goods companies. He was living out his goal of making lots of money and now dreamed of retiring at a young age. Then, in 1998, Rich's office phone rang. It was a headhunter looking for his recommendations as to who should lead World Vision.

The Stearns had been giving to World Vision for almost twenty years. They were both well aware of the organization and its Christian work. Rich figured he had gotten this call based on the family's giving record.

"The headhunter described the job and its challenges," Rich explained. "He then asked if I knew anyone who might be interested in filling the position. This job was part Mother Teresa, part Indiana Jones, and part CEO, and I couldn't think of anyone. Finally he asked me, 'What about you?' I laughed and explained I knew nothing about fundraising. That is where the call ended, but then the Holy Spirit began to prod me. I received another call, and again I told the caller I was not qualified or interested.

"When Reneé and I were engaged, she told me we had to go to the department store and register. I thought she was kidding. I didn't know about such things. When I found out she meant registering for our china, crystal, and silver, I told her that as long as there were children starving in the world, we were not going to have china, crystal, or silver. In an impossible twist of irony, twenty years later I became the CEO of Lenox, one of the world's largest producers of china, crystal, and silver. It was like a mirror being held up in front of my face and a voice saying,

'If you are still that same man, if you still care about those kids, then I have a job for you to do.' What were the chances, a billion to one? It had to be the Lord's plan. Finally in April 1998 I had dinner with the people from World Vision and, after much prayer, felt moved to give up all I had and take the job."

Over the past three decades, Rich and Reneé Stearns have realized the vision both of them had for themselves when they first met. It's just framed a bit differently than Rich Stearns could have ever imagined.

"You know," Rich marveled, "Reneé took a person who had grown up in a broken home, who had very little character, and who had dubious prospects. Yet she saw something in me. She knew that through faith I could be a better man. Thanks to her integrity, character, and standards, I became more than I should have been. The Lord knows, I am what I am because of her influence."

On that first date, Rich Stearns saw Jesus in Reneé's eyes and in her life. He didn't know what the light in her eyes meant then and he didn't recognize Christ as anything but a historical figure, but that look in her eyes kept drawing him back. Finally on a dark night when he was alone, he began to understand Reneé and himself. What he'd seen in the young woman's life forced him to look into his own heart. Shocking himself, he found Jesus waiting there for him.

16

I Keep My Eyes on You

Cynthia Clawson

Gospel Singer and Christian Speaker

Billboard magazine has called Cynthia Clawson "the most awesome voice in gospel music." The Texan's long list of awards include a Grammy and five Doves. Almost four decades into her career, she is still equally popular in churches and concerts, and has been featured many times as a part of the Gaither Homecoming concert series. This incredible vocalist has taken stages as varied as Robert Schuller's *Hour of Power* to London's Wembley Stadium. To call Cynthia dynamic is an understatement. Her voice does more than fill a room; it touches souls. Through her voice and testimony she has reached millions of people throughout the world with God's message of love and grace. For many, listening to Cynthia is like having a direct line to heaven's jukebox.

Clawson's path to stardom is one of the most interesting in contemporary Christian music. Beginning at age three Cynthia was featured in church and school. She sang all through high school and majored in vocal performance and piano at Howard

Payne University. Winning the Arthur Godfrey Talent Show led to her headlining on *CBS Newcomers*, a 1971 summer replacement for the *Carol Burnett Show*. Clawson's showmanship and vocal talents on TV landed her a recording contract. Record producer Red Buryl then used Cynthia as the featured vocalist in Ragan Courtney's album *Celebrate Life*. Within six months of that album project, Ragan and Cynthia were married, thus beginning a lifetime of creative collaboration and Christian outreach.

While most Christian artists have been professionally limited by the religious nature of their music, Cynthia has seen doors open from coast to coast to celebrate her Christ-filled recordings. Her rendition of "Softly and Tenderly" set the evocative tone for the soundtrack of the Academy Award–winning movie *The Trip to Bountiful*. In 1998 she recorded a cast album of gospel songs for a revival of the musical *Smoke on the Mountain*, which opened at the Lambs Theatre in New York City. Flying in the face of logic, Clawson's inspirational recordings have exposed her to millions. Unconventional? Yes! But Cynthia has always walked to her own drummer in her work and in her life.

For most people, the demands of being a successful singer and songwriter would be more than enough to fill the day. Yet Cynthia's life and work just begins with "making a joyful noise." Clawson and her husband are also the copastors of the Sanctuary Church in Austin, Texas. Their church doors are open to any who seek comfort, peace, and hope. So not only does she sing the good news, she teaches and preaches it as well. She finds no boundaries in being God's servant and therefore sees no limits in whom God sends to influence and touch her life. Thus, one of the most dynamic Christian lessons Cynthia learned was presented through a man others sought to exclude from God's kingdom and His church. Yet for Cynthia to see Jesus' face in the eyes of an outcast, a woman named Willie had to first touch Clawson's life.

Willie initially taught her granddaughter, Cynthia, about action. The woman was an energetic dynamo at home and at church. She didn't wait for others to do a job she could do herself. If Sunday school needed a teacher, she was there with her Bible in hand. If someone needed to be contacted for the church, she was in the car and on the way to the house before others could even look up the address. If someone needed a shoulder to cry on, she was there too. And if anything from cleaning the church bathrooms to organizing the songbooks needed attention, on a moment's notice Willie would be there to do the job. She knew that the Lord's work, just like all other jobs, didn't get done unless there were folks willing to do it. So she was always willing. Yet while her energy and action were obvious to everyone, there were some much more subtle qualities she also passed on to Cynthia.

"My grandmother Willie Eliza Pouncy Willbanks Patrick was the most influential Christian in my childhood," Cynthia recalled. "First of all, she taught me patience and acceptance. There were three very important deaths in her adult life. She faithfully accepted each. In 1948 her son suddenly died. A month later her husband passed away. Then, eight years later, her second husband died."

While the world around her seemed to constantly fall apart, Miss Willie did not waver. She remained the rock in her home and in her church. In the face of tragedy after tragedy she steadfastly believed that God was in control.

"The pastor of her church came up to her at her second husband's funeral," Cynthia recalled. "He told her, 'Miss Willie, you take some time off and come back to church when you are ready.' She immediately answered, 'I will be back as soon as possible.' She was back the next Sunday too!"

The power and meaning of her grandmother's Christian service made a tremendous impact on Cynthia. Not only did Willie serve, but she also reached out to men, women, and children whom others dismissed as being weird or not the right kind of person to be a part of a good Christian church.

Willie did not judge. She did not see that as part of her earthly job. If someone from a sordid background needed help, she was there for them. She didn't worry about their reputations or past indiscretions; she believed they were her Christian brothers and sisters and they should be respected, loved, and embraced just like everyone else. She knew the meaning of "the least of these" and lived it as she felt Christ would have wished her to every day of her life.

Many people who had been ignored by other Christians saw Jesus for the first time in Willie's eyes and actions. As these cast-out people were touched by this gentle woman, Cynthia responded too. From her earliest years she knew she wanted to reflect the compassion and courage of conviction she saw in her grandmother's life. As an adult and one of America's best-known Christian voices, she would find herself having to stand up with the same kind of courage of conviction when offering Christian friendship and comfort to one of her musicians.

"Raymond Brown was a songwriter and singer." Cynthia's voice lowered a bit as she recalled the events that have become so important in her life. "He and my husband wrote musicals together. Raymond played in my band with me. Yet from the beginning he was an odd duck. No one seemed to understand him, but I came to love him so.

"He looked like Oscar Wilde. Raymond had a large nose, odd-shaped body, a musician's long unkempt hair, blue eyes, curly kind of eyelashes, and skinny legs. I met him when he was a college student at Oklahoma Baptist University. He was a part of the cast of *Hello World*."

Cynthia's soon-to-be husband Ragan had written *Hello World*, and Raymond was a minor player in the large cast. In order to get noticed, Raymond constantly found reasons to talk to the director. Ragan enjoyed the young man's exuberance and even offhandedly told the student to come see him if he ever made it to New York. Raymond took the casual invitation literally. A few months later "the odd duck" knocked on Ragan's door and ended up staying with the writer for several months.

During his time in the Big Apple, Raymond became a member of the cast of Ragan's next musical, *Celebrate Life*, and toured the country with the production. He met Cynthia on that national tour. Even though he was strange and off-the-wall, Cynthia liked Raymond from the first meeting. Yet at that time she didn't have a clue their relationship would quickly become almost like family. When Cynthia married Ragan, she discovered that Raymond was essentially a part of the package. The young man soon became her piano player. While he fit in fine with the band, Cynthia's friends were not impressed.

Several times Cynthia was asked to keep Raymond out of sight. It was all right for him to play piano, but he usually wasn't welcome at social functions. Some found him ugly or badly dressed, others pointed out that he didn't have any social skills, and others were turned off by his personality. Once, when Cynthia was told to leave the "clown" at home because the party was too formal for folks like him, Cynthia did as instructed. Yet she expressed her loyalty to her pianist by wearing a clown suit to the fashionable get-together.

"In a way I think I sold out a little," Clawson remembered. "My grandmother would have just told them that if Raymond wasn't invited, she wasn't coming either. I would probably do that now, but at the time dressing up like a clown was my way of making a point."

As Raymond continued to pound the keyboards at her appearances and recording sessions, Cynthia continued to support him and offer God's compassion. As it turned out, soon he would need that and so much more.

In the early 1990s Raymond approached Ragan and Cynthia. He didn't look well. He seemed even more frail than normal. In a soft voice, Raymond informed the couple he had AIDS. Ragan and Cynthia were shocked to the core. But their response spoke volumes. The Clawsons made Raymond an even greater part of their family. Along with their children, and even Cynthia's extended family, they brought the man into a world of love and understanding he had never before known.

"The last Christmas we had with Raymond was in 1992," Cynthia recalled. "Grandmother was with us for that Christmas."

Willie observed the fragile man, visited with him, and shared a few holiday memories. When he grew tired, Ragan helped Raymond toward the door to take him home. Not hesitating for a moment, Willie got up from her chair, walked across the room, and gave the sick man a huge hug. After telling him "Merry Christmas," she silently watched him walk out to the car. The elderly woman paused for a moment to observe the fragile man painfully sit down. She then turned to her granddaughter.

"Does he have AIDS?" she asked. After Cynthia nodded, the old woman thought about the news, then added, "Those things just happen."

"That was a remarkable Christmas," Clawson recalled. "Raymond's family had pretty much disowned him, so we became the only family he had. My parents showed a lot of their faith that year. They knew he was gay, but they continued to accept and welcome him anyway. Like my grandmother, they did not judge."

AIDS was still not a Christian cause at that moment. Most churches had not yet opened their hearts to those who suffered from this illness. At a time when many people urgently needed to feel the hand of Christian compassion, love, and acceptance, some believers were acting much like those who demanded that the woman at the well be stoned. So judgments were overruling hearts, and few were willing to spend time with a gay man like Raymond.

For Cynthia these days were especially tough. She had always defended her friend. She didn't always understand him, but she would not judge him and she would not let others judge him either. Rather she prayed with him, held his hand, continually told him how much God loved him. And tried to get her friends to come see him as well.

"At that time Raymond was so many different things to me," she recalled. "Though he was only a little younger than me, he was one of my children, my brother, my teacher. So it was very difficult to watch him wither away. Yet that is what he did."

Raymond had never been a beautiful human being. Many had trouble looking at him when he was well. Now few could bare even to glance down at him. His body was so emaciated he looked like a concentration camp victim. Sores covered his skin, and his gums were cracked and bleeding.

"Eventually he couldn't speak," Cynthia painfully explained. "He would write notes to us. One of his notes asked, 'Is this the end?'"

Ragan read the note, looked over at his wife, and then back at Raymond. In a halting voice Ragan replied, "Yes, it is."

"At that moment," Cynthia continued, "Raymond began to cry. He wrote another note asking us to wipe his tears. When his tears had been wiped away and I looked again at this man, I felt as if I was looking at the face of Jesus. At that moment Raymond was the most beautiful person I had ever seen, and it was because Christ was in his eyes.

"Raymond's family had walked away from him some years before. When he needed them most, they were not there for him. Yet when he grew sickest, his mother and dad came. It was strange; his father would come to the hospital, but not inside."

Mr. Brown would sit alone in his car in the parking lot. Every day he would stare blankly out the windshield trying to come to grips with what was going on a few hundred feet away. Finally, when his son's time was numbered in hours, he summoned the courage to open the car door, walk into the building, and take the elevator up to Raymond's room. He nervously strolled in and looked into his dying son's eyes. The big welder searched for words but could only manage to hug his frail boy and whisper, "Daddy loves Raymond." This was the final bit of closure Raymond Brown needed. He peacefully died soon after that needed embrace.

Seeing the face of Jesus reflected in Raymond's eyes both haunted Cynthia and brought her peace. From that look she knew the Lord had been with her pianist in his final moments. And He had been there to do more than just pave the way for Raymond's trip home. Jesus had also been there to show the singer what her grandmother had long known: the work must continue.

"From the day I saw Raymond reflecting Christ in his eyes," Cynthia explained, "until this very moment, I still see Raymond everywhere. When I see someone in trouble, a young lady walking by herself down the highway, a homeless man living under a bridge, I am reminded of Raymond. Because in that bed, helpless and alone, he was the least of these. And because of all of his eccentricities, I don't judge people by their exterior. I just try to find the good God has placed in their hearts, then reach out to them with the blessings He has given me."

Since Raymond's death, Cynthia has also established a tradition that keeps Raymond's testimony alive even after his voice had been stilled. She has concluded her concerts with an incredible gospel song penned by her unique friend in his final years. Raymond wrote "I Keep My Eyes on You" to show others that no matter how difficult life became, faith would carry them through.

Meanwhile, Cynthia's Grandma Willie lived until 1993, continuing about the Lord's business, not stopping to judge but always pausing to help. And she continued to tell her granddaughter, "What you were is not important. What is important is allowing the Lord to use you now."

Recently Cynthia released another powerful testimony in song. *See Me, God* has received an incredible audience. The material in this album explores the struggles and sorrows of life, as it celebrates the faith and joy that result from this struggle. No doubt the inspiration for much of this very personal project came from a grandmother and a piano player who together taught Cynthia to always reach out, never judge, never quit working for the Lord, and never be surprised at whose eyes she sees Jesus in.

17

Seeing Freedom behind Bars

Terri Blackstock

Bestselling Author

Terri Blackstock is a small woman whose talent, wisdom, and depth cast a giant shadow. This bestselling Christian author is focused, vivacious, dynamic, driven, bright, and outgoing. Her smile lights up a room, and her charm seems capable of calming a storm. She is currently renowned for penning chart-topping book series such as Cape Refuge, Suncoast Chronicles, and Newpointe 911. This incredible inspirational success makes the second time Terri has been lauded as a premier novelist. Ten years ago she was an award-winning secular author with a resume including thirty-two titles and 3.5 million books sold. So Terri's talent and passion for writing are unquestionable; even the toughest critics recognize the petite lady is a giant in her field. Yet there is far more to this woman than just the sum of her book sales.

In 1982, when Terri began her literary journey, she composed sexy, romantic thrillers. While this type of writing made her well known and brought in regular royalty checks, she found herself disillusioned. As a lukewarm Christian, a young wife who had been raised in the church but had drifted away from any kind of passionate involvement with her faith, she rationalized her liberal use of sex as a means to an end. She convinced herself she was giving readers what they wanted and that for her readers her work was an escape, not a moral roadmap. So day after day she confidently wrote on. In 1990, after a divorce, that confidence suddenly drained away, and she began to question every element of her life. The confused and now single writer moved back to her Jackson, Mississippi, hometown to try to find some answers.

"The breakup of my marriage," Terri recalls, "was a terrible tragedy for me, but I now believe God used it to help me turn back to Him. I moved back to my hometown, where I found a church that offered a divorce recovery ministry and an active singles program. Through that ministry, I began getting my life back on track."

As she found her way back to her faith, Terri continued to turn out steamy novels. Yet at the same time she also began to study the Bible and forge relationships with men and women involved in mission outreach at every level.

"I met my husband, Ken, through the church," Terri explained. "We married in 1992. Two years later, Ken realized he had never had more than an intellectual knowledge of Jesus. It was then he came to know Christ as his Lord and Savior. He thus became the spiritual leader that I had yearned for all my life."

Ken's giving his body and soul to the Lord stoked a new fire of desire in Terri. She wanted what her husband had. Ultimately she saw that the obstacle between herself and her Savior was the type of books she was writing.

"It didn't matter how many people read my work," Terri admitted, "if I couldn't tell them what I knew. If I couldn't tell them what would solve their problems and change their lives, it was of no good."

At this point the writer walked away from her livelihood and her large fan base. Taking a huge leap of faith, she cut ties with her secular publishers. She even had to buy back several romance projects she had agreed to write but had not yet started.

"We had already spent the money I'd been paid in advances," Terri explained. "But the Lord provided an answer. It turned out my publishers owed me more money than I owed them."

With the contracts resolved, she moved on to new writing goals. "I wanted to start with something fresh because I was really tired of romance," she recalled. "I submitted a proposal to Zondervan, and before I knew it, I was offered a contract for four books."

Terri's move to Christian fiction contained none of the roadblocks she had feared. But her journey to discover a mission of faith in her own life was a bit more difficult. In fact, on first glance, the couple who would mentor her growth as they mirrored Jesus in word and deed seemed more like characters created in a work of fiction than folks who were a regular part of the congregation at her church.

Nicki and Dick Benz did not appear to be models of Christian servitude. Dick was a gruff cowboy type. In Jackson he seemed bigger than life, someone who'd be more at home on a West Texas range than a southern plantation. His voice was loud, his handshake was firm, and his personality embraced a no-nonsense approach to life. Dick was so tough that a casual observer would have never realized that under his large chest was a heart as soft as butter.

Dick's wife was tiny, almost fragile, like a delicate flower. This retired woman didn't look like a fearless woman of action who constantly looked for new challenges. She looked like someone who might stay home and pray, who might even visit a sick friend, but not one who would inspire a movement touching hundreds of women who often walked on the wrong side of the law.

"Before I met them," Terri explained, "Dick was a good guy, but he was not on fire for the Lord. Then, several years ago, he had a heart attack. He spent two weeks in ICU waiting for surgery. During that time he did business with God. When he came out of the hospital, he was a changed man."

With a second lease on life, Dick dove into Christian service with a vigor that overwhelmed all who knew him. Two days a week he ran a benevolence ministry at his church to help those down on their luck with bills, food, clothing, and housing. Through hard work and determination he came up with an ever-growing base of support for his dynamic mission. Yet while Dick was busy touching the least of these on the streets, his wife was looking in another area. Her vision would not only dramatically change this couple's focus but for Terri Blackstock would bring Christian service alive in a new way.

"Nicki and Dick were watching a local news story about prostitutes," Terri explained. "The interviews deeply touched Nicki's heart. She was overwhelmed when she considered these women's hopeless lives."

Others would have soon dismissed the tragic stories and moved on to something else, but not the diminutive Mrs. Benz. She started praying about a way she could touch the prostitutes with hope and compassion. She ultimately decided the best way to reach them was to go to jail!

"Nicki got in touch with the sheriff," Terri recalled. "When she got permission to visit with incarcerated prostitutes, nothing could stop her. Imagine, a woman who had never been to a jail, had never known a prostitute, walking into that environment. On that day, with a Bible in her hand, she introduced herself to the inmates. Then after she explained she had been led to reach out to them, she began a Bible study."

The prostitutes and drug addicts who met Nicki that day had to be shocked. Why would this woman be interested in them? After all, no one else was. On that first meeting, most of the women probably didn't take her very seriously. Yet the fact that no one suddenly reformed during her first trip to jail did not faze Nicki. The next week she surprised the jailers and the prisoners when she came back again.

"She would go to the jail week after week," Terri explained, "and she fell in love with those women. She would lead them in Bible studies and bless them. She placed chocolate in their hands and said, 'Did you know you are God's treasure? God sent me to tell you He loves you and so do I.' Then she would pray with them. She wasn't judging them or preaching to them; she was there to give them worth."

This tiny woman was going behind bars to minister to thieves, hookers, and drug dealers. She was trying to break down walls and reach people who had rarely heard a kind word or felt a gentle touch. On the surface it shouldn't have worked. This little grandmother type having an impact on young women who lived on the streets would have been too outlandish for Blackstock to write into a novel. Yet as the weeks turned to months, those who worked at the jail noted a gradual change in the inmate population. Some began to appear to be happy. Bible study was common, and many couldn't wait to spend time with Mrs. Benz.

"When she walks in the room Christ glows within her." Terri's voiced showed awe as she tried to find the words to fully describe Nicki and her spirit. "The whole room seems to light up. When she is talking to you, the look in her eyes makes you feel like you are the only person in the world. When she first talked to me about these woman, her eyes glistened with tears because she was so moved and so serious about the women in the jail."

Terri and a few others from church got so caught up in Nicki's stories that they asked to go with her. For Terri the experience was overwhelming. The flawed people she was trying to bring to life in her books, those struggling to find answers for their lives, were the very ones Nicki was touching each week.

"I discovered these women have great needs," Terri explained. "I met mothers who needed to have us check on their children. I met one lady who should have been released a month before, but no one was letting her out. These women had no voice, and because of that, they had no sense of worth. Yet Nicki was giving them both of those things."

At first Dick didn't get involved in the jail ministry. For reasons that went all the way back to his childhood, he was not comfortable with it. The hurdle he had to climb in order to accept and love these women would inspire Terri as much as had the compassionate look in Nicki's eyes.

"Dick had always been a racist," Terri recalled. "He'd always had a very low opinion of people of other races. Many of the women whom Nicki was visiting were African-American. So, before Dick could get involved in the jail ministry, a very large wall had to be torn down. His eyes had to be opened so he could understand that all men and women were the same in the Lord's eyes."

Terri watched Dick as he listened to his wife's stories and observed her zeal for this mission. As a husband he wanted to support her, but it was difficult for him to accept those his wife was reaching. Yet through prayer and a lot of personal reflection, Dick came to an understanding that he had been wrong about race for his entire life. As if a blindfold had been removed, Dick now looked at all men and women as more than just a part of the family of God; they were members of his family as well.

Seeing God make this change in Dick's life all but over-whelmed Terri. As she looked into the old cowboy's eyes, she now saw the same reflection of Jesus she had observed in Nicki. If God could make this kind of impact in this couple's lives, then their ministry was something the writer knew she had to embrace too.

When Nicki had first started going to the jail, they wouldn't let any men accompany her to visit the women. So Nicki would bring home a list of the women's needs, things like calling their families, finding them a drug rehab, calling their public defenders, and getting them a pair of glasses, and Dick would take the list and start making phone calls. Nicki said that for every hour she spent at the jail, Dick spent forty keeping all the promises she'd made to the inmates. Everntually, Dick called the sherriff's department and convinced them to let him start going to the jail with Nicki. They finally agreed.

When he went to the jail for the first time, his devotion, compassion, and love for both his wife and the Lord reflected the image of a godly husband. Many prisoners had never before encountered this type of man. Not only were many of the inmates overwhelmed, but when Dick saw their reaction and felt their pain, he was moved as well.

When any of the women were released from the facility, Dick found them places to live and to work. The old cowboy became an advocate, demanding that his Christian friends give some of these women a second chance. Yet the couple did not stop there.

"Dick and Nicki started Buried Treasures Ministry," Terri explained. "They had seen many fail on the streets because of living in a bad environment and getting caught up in old habits. So they began to take some of the women who had been released from jail into their home. If someone was getting out of jail, they opened their doors to them. They take in up to four women at a time. And this is not a very big home, under two thousand square feet. For the time that they live with Nicki and Dick, these women don't work. Instead they spend their time in Bible study and working with Dick in the church's benevolence ministry. After a few months, they can attend the local community college to learn job skills. At home there is a lot of nurturing going on too."

Going into a jail, acting as advocates, finding jobs, and opening up their home to ex-cons would have been more than enough for most retired couples. But for Nicki and Dick it was just a foundation. They began to reach out to the children of the inmates. To show these kids they had not been forgotten, the couple organized back-to-school drives to buy clothes and supplies. At Christmas they even have a party where Nicki and Dick, with the help of many volunteers and donors from their church, sponsor activities, clowns, decorations, and food, as well as tell the story of the birth of Jesus. At the end of the party they give away presents. One year each of the more than two hundred children at the party received a bicycle.

"If you are in jail," Terri explained, "you are separated from the world. It is easy to forget that anyone cares. Nicki and Dick understand that better than most. Each woman in jail gets a very special gift from the couple. Nicki and Dick take pictures of the inmates' families and give them to the prisoners. When they hold those photos in their hands and stare at them, they sob. When that happens all of us who are there melt."

More than two thousand years ago, when Christ was hung on a cross, on each side of Him were two thieves. In all the pain and suffering, the Lord could have ignored them, but He didn't. He sought to comfort and assure them they were not forgotten. In Jackson, Mississippi, in a slightly different way, a retired couple is reaching out and paving the road to salvation and success for a new generation of forgotten prisoners.

"Nicki and Dick's eyes see so much in people," Terri explains. "In fact, they see with God's eyes. They see beyond the appearance to the heart. They see potential. They see with the Holy Spirit's eyes."

Nicki and Dick Benz did more than bring Terri into a ministry; they brought her a new understanding of the promise found in flawed people, the very ones who are the stars of her books. Through the example of Nicki and Dick, the author now understands the potential she has to touch every person who reads one of her books with her stories of hope, faith, compassion, and redemption. It is a message Terri says with words, but one Nicki and Dick say with actions and through the look in their eyes.

18

The Grace in a Mother's Eyes

Don Reid

Member of the Statler Brothers, Inspirational Author

For three and a half decades, from debut to departure, Don Reid was a member of one of the most recognized vocal groups in the history of music. The Statler Brothers were originals, unlike anything that had come before or has come since. Much more than just singers, they were storytellers who spun their tales in rhyme and harmony. And a majority of their songs that became chart-topping hits looked into the elements of life that everyone else seemed to forget. Don, Harold, Phil, Lew, and later Jimmy wrote like Norman Rockwell painted; they captured rich snapshots of America's simplest scenes and preserved them in an unforgettable musical form.

On records and in concerts, the Statler Brothers made people smile, cry, look back at special moments or people, and even caused a few folks to think. With hits like "The Class of '57," "Flowers on the Wall," "Did You Know You Are My Sunshine," and "More

Than a Name on the Wall," Don and the boys from Staunton, Virginia, would imprint a lasting and emotional impression on the United States. And while they would spend more than thirty years traveling coast to coast and border to border, their home address would always remain their birthplace, and Don and his partners would also hold onto the spiritual roots of their childhood.

"My mother was the backbone of the family," Don explained as he looked back over a life that began in the Virginia hills in the concluding days of World War II. "There were three of us kids, and I know it sounds trite to say this, but she was a perfect mother. She had a great sense of what was important and always focused on those things."

Frances Reid was a pleasant woman with a big smile and a hearty hello. At first glance, this joyful mother appeared to have life pretty easy. She always had time to check in on friends, and she would volunteer for community, school, and church projects on a moment's notice. Yet looks are often deceiving. In fact Frances's life was anything but easy. She worked five nights a week, from eleven until seven, at a state mental institution. There in a world of misunderstood souls, she labored to bring hope and peace to broken men and women. Her gentle smile and kind words were often the only "Christian" touch many of these patients ever received.

"Besides doing the jobs of a mother and a wife," Don remembered, "she worked at night, then slept in the daytime. Yet she wouldn't let us leave the house for school without spending some time with us. And she would always set her alarm so that she was up before we got home."

For the Reid children this sense of being important to their mother created a deep respect for her. They knew she worked hard, but they never sensed they finished second to her job. Because she made each of them feel of great value, her children embraced the elements of her life that she considered to be most important.

"One of the first things I remember learning was that we always had to be at church. And she didn't send us; she took us. She didn't just sit in the pew either. As early as I can remember she was a Sunday school teacher and a leader in vacation Bible school. She was ready to do any job that needed doing. In fact, she was the first woman in our Presbyterian church to be approached to be an elder. Ironically she didn't believe a woman should fill this role, so she turned it down. But that is just the kind of pillar she was in our church. So I indeed knew that church was very important."

Yet at the Reid home a Christian life did not begin and end when the church doors opened and closed. In fact, the Lord was just as alive in their tiny home as He was under the big steeple downtown. And Frances made sure the Lord's lessons were taught day in and day out, through each and every one of life's experiences.

"She did everything quietly," Don explained. "She never preached to you, but she taught you the lessons you needed to know by example or suggestion."

Mother Reid's Bible was not just read every day; it was studied. Her children watched her as she pulled out pencils and pens, underlined favorite Scriptures, and jotted down notes on the sides of the pages. And she then looked for ways to apply those lessons to her children's lives.

Don grew up in the segregated South. In the early- and mid-fifties the idea of integration had not hit yet the rural areas.

So it was rare to see children from different races associating with one another. The rules of society prevented it.

"I remember one day after vacation Bible school I wanted to play softball. So I rode my bike down to the field. When I got there some black kids were playing on the field. I watched them for a while, then got back on my bike and went home."

When Don arrived at home, he said nothing. He just strolled into the house, tossed his glove in a chair, and sat down.

"I thought you were going to play some softball," Frances inquired.

"I wanted to," Don replied, "but the black kids were already there."

His mother paused for a moment, looking up from her cleaning, then asked a question that was not meant to be answered. "What's wrong, don't they play ball too?"

Don didn't answer, but he thought about what she said. Yes, they were playing ball, he told himself. Looking back at his mother, staring deeply into her eyes, a simple truth suddenly hit him. There was no reason not to join that game.

As the years went by Don realized that his mother was trying to teach him to look beyond color and into a person's heart. She believed that when he did, he would find a great deal in common with everyone he met.

"She was amazing with how she taught us," he explained. "She didn't preach, didn't scold, she just put everything in its place, and at the same time she put me in my place. That was her charm. Often, just a look down over the top of her glasses was all she needed to teach us what we needed to know."

On that long-ago summer day Don jumped back on his bike, went back to the ball diamond, and asked the kids on the field if he could play too. Without realizing it, a decade before the local schools opened their doors to African-Americans, the boy took a large step toward integration. That step was taken because his mother felt a need to teach her son an important Christian lesson. That teaching wouldn't stop at this monumental moment; it would continue day after day, week after week, and year after year.

It might have been her work at the mental institution, a place filled with people of all races and backgrounds, or maybe it was just something she learned through Bible study, but Frances had a real understanding of all people being God's children. As he grew older Don began to notice this too. He watched his mother as she sincerely tried to live as Christ had. She didn't judge, she didn't separate, she didn't choose who she associated with based on class, race, or distinction, and she wouldn't allow her children to stoop to doing any of those things either. She opened her heart and home to anyone who needed a hand or a prayer. Therefore her life lessons took hold and rooted deeply in her children's hearts.

Because church was so important in the Reid household, music was an important facet of spiritual growth. Through youth choirs and community singings, Don and his older brother Harold were exposed to a rich library of gospel music. In high school the brothers joined with friends Lew DeWitt and Philip Balsley to form a local quartet. Singing songs such as "Amazing Grace" and "Just a Little Talk with Jesus," the Kingsmen, as they called themselves, began to work up an enthusiastic local following. Until they were discovered by Johnny Cash, no one expected the boys ever to do much more than charm regional audiences. Yet when the country music superstar took the boys on the road and they changed their name to the Statler Brothers, the quartet quickly made noise on both the country and rock charts. In just a few years the kids from Staunton grew into one of the most important vocal groups in country music since the Sons of the Pioneers.

The Statler Brothers' journey to the top was really due to the hand-penned hits that reflected the middle-American values and life lessons taught by Don and Harold's mother. In no small way, these "Sunday school" lessons also were the reason that each of the four refused to get caught up in the lure of stardom. They stubbornly did not change their personalities, their values, or even their addresses. Nowhere was this adherence to lessons taught by Frances Reid more apparent than in the group's obvious Christian witness.

One in every ten songs that the Statler Brothers recorded was a hymn or gospel standard. You simply couldn't purchase a Statler Brothers album without getting a dose of sincere faith at the same time. This recording formula could be traced back to their mother's practice of tithing not just financially but with her time and talents too.

In concerts, no matter the makeup of the crowd or the venue, the group also devoted a portion of every show to religious music. It wasn't a token gesture either. Don was simply singing hymns the way his mother had taught him, with every bit of sincere emotion he could force from his soul. Folks who had a much different idea of right and wrong than did the Reids were not dismissed during this portion of the performance. As their mother had taught them, being different does not give any of us cause to ignore people or not reach out to them. Hymns went out to believer and nonbeliever alike, and the line between the two was often erased because of the message found in the lyrics. Even though some of the crowd might have imbibed in a different kind of spirit before a show, they could not help but note the Spirit in the group's gospel standards.

Yet even more remarkable for a group which year after year crisscrossed the country performing more than two hundred shows annually was the men's insistence on being in church on Sunday morning. When the church bells were ringing, no matter where they were, the guys were in their suits and ready to worship.

"When we were growing up we always went to church," Don recalled. "So even when we were touring, on Sunday morning we would get up and find a church to attend. It didn't make any difference where we were, we would find a place to join with others and worship. If you weren't in church on Sunday, it just felt like you were skipping. And Harold and I knew that Mom wouldn't stand for that."

In fact, from time to time, even after Don had children of his own, his mother would track him down on Sunday afternoon and make sure he had been to church somewhere that morning. When she was in her eighties, she still checked to make sure her boys were keeping their date with the Lord each Sunday.

Frances was there the first time her boys performed as a quartet, and in 2003 she was there the last time the Statler Brothers took the concert stage. It was a career that began and ended with "Amazing Grace."

"She was such a strong influence," Don explained. "I think she deserves the credit for much of the success I have had. When she died I inherited her Bible, the one she wrote her notes in, and I go to it quite often. So she is still teaching me, she is still guiding my way in life." So much so that the former stage star has penned two Christian books reflecting on his small-town faith: *Sunday Morning Memories* and *Heroes and Outlaws of the Bible: Down Home Reflections of History's Most Colorful Men and Women.*

In 1979, in the middle of the group's incredible career, the Statler Brothers hit the top ten with a song called "Nothing As Original As You." For most who heard this number it was just another clever Statler Brothers standard, but for Don it was probably more. So many times he had looked into his mother's eyes and realized that God was looking at him through her. The Lord was teaching him through her example. And He was telling him that each of His children are originals, each has gifts, each has talents, and each has the opportunity for grace. Don first found that grace in his mother's eyes and at his mother's church. That grace was always there waiting for him when he got home from school as a child. Thanks to his understanding of the Lord's love as displayed through his mother's touch, Don Reid came to understand that grace was also wherever he went on the road as a part of the amazing Statler Brothers. That grace had been in his mother's eyes when he was born, and it remains in his heart today.

19

Off the Beaten Path

Crystal Bowman
Author and Speaker

Faith is tested not when things are good but when people face challenges. When life is the toughest, character is exposed; conversely when life is at its best, selfishness often rears its ugly head. Harold Langejan would face a series of horrible breaks at an age when his world should have been filled with fun and games. His faith shone through on each occasion. Yet even more remarkably, when his life became filled with many blessings, his eyes looked outward, searching for ways to share his blessings with others. Reaching back to his own past and experiences, Herk, as his friends called him, would build a bridge of faith to channel his good fortune to the "least of these." In doing so he did more than just share the gospel and lift a small community; he forever changed his daughter's life.

Herk was the eighth of nine children born to a Michigan farmer and his wife in the dynamic and colorful 1920s. What should have been an idyllic life filled with fishing, biking, and school, changed abruptly due to the Great Depression. With the older Langejan children now grown and gone, Herk had to quit school and devote ten to twelve hours a day to hard labor on the family farm. In the cold blizzards of winter or the hot humid days of summer, he did a man's job, never complaining, never once asking why he had been forced to give up so much while his friends lived out their lives as normal teenagers.

In America, just as it had been for generations in the Langejan's ancestral home of Holland, family was placed ahead of everything. This meant always pulling together in times of great need. When Herk's sister delivered her first child, the young teenager walked fifteen miles through the Michigan snow to do the new mother's chores. A few months later when another sister's husband suddenly died, Herk took over the farm duties, and though just a young teen, became a surrogate father for his nieces and nephews.

The years of hard work made the boy strong and determined, and the responsibilities he undertook forced him to be self-disciplined, yet bad times could not take away his quick smile or the twinkle in his eye. And the messages he heard at the community church gave him the faith to believe that something special was just around the corner. All he had to do was continue praying and keep looking.

In the bright days just before World War II, Herk, a good-looking young man in need of money, took an extra job picking strawberries. A pretty young girl was working in the fields that day. Langejan charmed the innocent beauty with his wit while his hands helped her fill her buckets with strawberries. This simple act of kindness would bloom into love. Yet before he could marry the woman of his dreams, war broke out, and Herk was drafted into the army. He used a weekend pass and married his sweetheart, then left home for three and a half years. If he was bitter about the long time he spent serving his country and separated from his bride, his letters didn't show it. And when he did come back, the smile on his face and the prayer of thankfulness on his lips convinced friend and family alike that nothing could change Herk's positive outlook.

During the course of the war, Herk's father-in-law had died. Rather than simply take his mother-in-law's daughter away to live with him, Herk constructed two homes side by side: one for his bride, another for her mother. And this was just the beginning of his building career. Using skills learned in his youth on the farm, Herk created a successful construction business. He lived by the motto of "No job too little or too large." Through hard work, long hours, and incredible determination, he supported his three daughters and a son. The middle daughter was named Crystal.

"When I was growing up," Crystal said, "I thought my father was one of the strongest, handsomest men in the world. He was five foot ten, probably about one hundred and eighty pounds, and had a lot of dark brown hair. His blue eyes had incredible life in them, and he always had a quick smile. He was warm, charming, and very comfortable to be with."

To anyone who saw them together it was obvious that Crystal idolized her dad. From the time she could walk she loved to be with the handsome businessman. As she grew older, his good looks and strong shoulders took a backseat to his actions.

"Our home was filled with a lot of love and compassion," Crystal recalled. "Dad had been raised Christian Reformed. He was active in his church all his life and made sure we were raised like he was. Dad allowed his love for the Lord to reflect in how he loved and treated us. As a parent he balanced strict rules with love and fun. He might have dished out some discipline, but it came with equal parts of love. So none of us rebelled against him, because we always sensed and felt his warmth.

"When I was in elementary school I began to notice that his love and compassion didn't end at home; he was just as generous with neighbors, relatives, friends, people from the church, and even strangers. If they needed something that was his, it was theirs for the asking. Folks were always borrowing his trucks, and he never charged them a dime. Everything he owned was available to whoever needed it. He also helped friends and extended family if they had a financial need, but he always did it in a quiet way so no one would know. I'm sure I will never know how many people he gave money to."

Crystal was also fascinated by her father's desire to share his love of the Lord with others. Long before she fully understood the power of faith, she realized how important it was to her father.

"Besides being kind and generous with friends and even strangers," Crystal remembered, "he had a burden for the lost and a passion for sharing the gospel. He would visit people in the hospital, sit beside their beds, and read Scripture to them. And if someone didn't respond, he wouldn't give up either. He would come back time and time again. He visited a dying atheist for days, right up until the moment he died. That is how important sharing his faith was to him."

Those he visited for his church or through his business were in Herk's line of sight. They were easy to see. It was when his deep eyes looked beyond his community to places few know of and even fewer had visited that his daughter learned the greatest lessons of faith.

"I don't know how he found it," Crystal explained, "but Dad discovered a forgotten rural neighborhood that was home to migrant workers and their families. It was hidden away, off on a dirt road, out of sight of the rest of the world, and yet for some reason, Dad took that road and found those people."

During his first visit to this place, the businessman must have been shocked. At the end of that unpaved, muddy road were tiny one- and two-room shacks filled with men, women, and children living with absolutely nothing. They earned what little they had picking blueberries, grapes, and apples. These Hispanic workers were living in Third World conditions right in the richest country in the world. There was no power or water and no city services. Not only were they out of sight of the prosperous world around them but they were cut off from it by both poverty and prejudice.

Most men would have simply shaken their heads and driven away. They might have said a prayer for the raggedly dressed children, might have even told others how horrible the conditions in the community were, but they wouldn't have come back again. Most would have said that because these people were from a different culture, someone else should help them. Yet Herk was not most people.

Herk saw in the faces of the children a face from his past. He knew, from his own experience, that these children had given up their childhoods to help their families make ends meet. Herk remembered what those long hours of hard work were like and knew that he only made it because of faith. Therefore rather than turn his back on these people, he sought out the man who owned the land where these folks lived. He bought a piece of property in that desperate community and constructed a church.

"I remember when he built the chapel," Crystal explained. "He found a preacher too. When he first started the ministry in that poor neighborhood, he felt he needed to connect with the people personally before they would be willing to come to church. He canvassed the dirt roads of the community on foot, inviting family after family to come to church. If they needed food or clothing, he distributed what they needed at the church service. He did this for many years regardless of weather, and the ministry flourished. He got others from the church and community involved as well. And because of my father's vision, several of these people who lived earthly lives of poverty have a mansion in glory."

Crystal often went with her father into this world of forgotten souls. She met the people and saw the haunting and hopeless looks in the eyes of the children who had nothing. And she witnessed how the acts of kindness and compassion put life, joy, and happiness into those eyes. With so many now joining her father in this mission of hope, the forgotten village became known, and its people found a bridge to the rest of the world.

As the Ike years of a comfortable America gave way to Kennedy and dreams of landing on the moon, the daughter noted that her father continued to keep his sights on those in need. Though he didn't know it then, Herk's devotion and determination to make a difference in God's name was making a lasting impression on Crystal.

"My father had always been kind and compassionate and especially cared about those who were needy or less fortunate. He was always willing to help out however and whenever he could. The passage from Matthew 25:37–40 makes me think of him.

When he cared for 'the least of these' he was doing it for the Lord. And I came to realize that was his motivation.

"He just had an eighth-grade education, yet he taught me how to make the most of my life. He used his gifts and abilities to become the best he could be. And he had such a work ethic, not just for his business, but for the Lord's work. I came to realize that my dad's purpose and calling were to serve the Lord. Therefore, on so many different occasions, I would see Jesus in his crystal clear blue eyes."

Crystal Bowman is a lyricist, poet, and author of thirty books. She earned a B.A. in elementary education from Calvin College, became a teacher, and studied early childhood development at the University of Michigan. She is active in the local schools of her Grand Rapids, Michigan, home, entertaining students with her poems and stories. She is a vital part of her church, even writing Bible study materials for women and children. Yet in her mind she does not do any of these things by herself. For Crystal not a day goes by that she doesn't see her father's Christ-filled eyes guiding her own walk of service. Due in no small part to her father, her goal is to lift up children, giving them hope and joy while leading them to the Lord.

"Dad taught me to be aware of the people around me," Crystal explained. "He taught me to use my eyes and look for opportunities to do the Lord's work. He taught me to care about everyone I meet."

While Crystal first saw Jesus in her father's eyes, in her own walk as a wife, mother, and successful children's writer, there can be no doubt that many have seen the Lord in her eyes as well. Faith passed down through love's action can live forever.

20

The Wright Way
Woody Wright
Gospel Singer,
Songwriter, Arranger

Beside a fork along an old, worn road, in a flat area between Heavenly Hollow and Bugger Bottom, a small, clear stream filled with cool, clean water runs by a simple country church. Many who know this creek well, those who live by it and use its crystal clear waters each day, believe that when the good Lord created the earth, He somehow found the time to reach down between the huge trees that lined the bank and let His hand linger in the waters. From that day till now, this quiet little stream has been special, a place of spiritual healing, a place of peace and tranquillity.

And for those reasons, as well as a few hundred more, a large number of the folks around the Kingston, Tennessee, area feel this flowing water contains special elements that are somehow tied to a healthy, productive life. For as long as anyone can remember, every Sunday before and after morning and evening services, church members would tarry on the banks studying the ripples, undercurrents, and deep channels. To these simple people, it seemed that looking into the shimmering pools immediately dissipated all of their concerns, thus putting the things of life that really mattered into perspective. It was as if they could cast their cares on the water and watch them all float away.

More than stare into the water, more than just admire its beauty, these people actually partook of it. Pulling old plastic and glass jugs from their pickup truck beds and car trunks, the members would lean down, fill the containers with the cool clear water, and take them home. It is still said that once you taste a refreshing sip of this water, it stays with you forever. It becomes a part of your life, your fabric and fiber. This special water doesn't just quench your thirst, it takes up residence in your soul. Its life, energy, and peace never leave your bloodstream. No matter where you go, it is always inside, reminding you of your roots and calling you home.

In the midsixties, a time when our nation was caught up in so many divisive issues, a gangly, dark-headed youngster often paused beside that stream to gaze into the deep pools before walking the final steps to the big wooden doors of the Cedar Grove Baptist Church. Woody Wright seemed to know that everything he needed in life could be found right here. In a world filled with so much hate and turmoil, this was a place of real peace that transcended understanding. And ten-year-old Woody somehow grasped this concept.

Even more than the stream, it was the church that called out to Woody. Most Sunday mornings his parents stayed home and he came by himself. He came because he knew that someone was waiting for him, always looking forward to seeing his smiling face. Each Sunday when he first entered the building a few minutes before Sunday school began, he heard a woman's happy voice almost always followed by a high-pitched giggle. He didn't fully understand why, but that greeting always brought a warm rush to his heart.

"She was already an old lady," he explained, his brown eyes sparkling with the same mischievous qualities that must have first endeared him to the Sunday school teacher, "but she always had the sweetest smile and the sweetest godly face I had ever seen. Her name was Billye Keylon, and she wore this long vest filled with perfect-attendance pins. It impressed me so much that she was always in Sunday school and, as the pins showed, had been there forever. As a kid I remember how it amazed me. She lived within walking distance from the church, and I mean if the doors were open and anybody was there, she was there too. And come snow or rain or whatever, she was there. There was no reason for not being at church. That was dedication. But even more than just the fact that she never let anything stop her from attending, it impressed me that she was always taking care of the kids. She wasn't with people her own age; she was with us. She seemed to have a special place in her heart for us, and I felt it immediately."

Mrs. Billye Keylon was one of the pillars of the Cedar Grove Baptist Church. Unlike so many others whose lives and viewpoints had grown more narrow with the passing years, she had remained young in thought and deed. She had refused to believe that getting up in years meant she wasn't supposed to grow or be in touch. She wouldn't watch the world pass her by. No, she just picked up her pace and tried to stay a few steps ahead of it.

Despite her slight build, gray hair, and thick granny glasses, this grandmotherly woman had dark sparkling eyes filled with enough energy to jumpstart even the most run-down, sleepy

Sunday morning soul. Her mind moved with the speed and grace of a world-class athlete, quickly and surely pulling children into her stories of mission work and Bible history with a fascination and curiosity they usually reserved for Saturday morning cartoons.

"She taught the young girls' Sunday school class," Woody recalled, then laughingly added, "and that's why most of the young boys hung around her a lot at first. But once we got around her, we discovered that she was such a neat lady we almost forgot about the girls."

In the process of chasing after those cute little girls, Woody discovered a woman who brought old stories to life. In one brief moment, with a hushed word or a wave of her hand, she could catch his attention and hold it. Then when they were all waiting on the edge of their seats, she'd smile and take them on a trip to another place and another time. When she told him about Noah, Woody could feel the boat rocking. When she spoke of Paul, he could picture the Roman roads on which he traveled. And when she told stories about Jesus, Woody felt as if he were looking directly into His eyes. Suddenly the Bible wasn't a dusty book that rested beside a bed; it was a wonderful technicolor adventure that came alive in his head and heart. When Mrs. Keylon told Bible stories, they became real.

Mrs. Keylon was more than just a teacher; she was a friend. No generation gap divided her from her students. She knew what was going on. She was aware of the music, styles, and news that interested her youngsters. And she used this knowledge to gain confidence and open doors to her Christian influence.

Recognizing that children were not going to come to her house if there was nothing to do, Mrs. Keylon and her husband stocked their refrigerator with soft drinks, their cabinets with snacks, and their closets with games. They also got out their shovels and dug a big hole in the front yard. Then after buying some concrete, pouring it, and letting it cure, they filled it with water from the creek that rolled gently by the church. Hot, dusty summer days now had a whole new meaning for the Sunday school kids. They had a pool!

In no time, Mrs. Keylon's influence on Woody began to reach out and touch others through him. His family came from a strong Christian background but had not been involved in church since moving to Kingston in the early sixties. But with their son so involved and having so much fun, they became more than a little curious about what was going on down there. In order to find out why Woody was so excited about getting up early every Sunday morning, they began to attend too. In no time they were hooked. And they were not alone.

Many families who had once just dropped their kids off at the church's front door began to wander inside with them. Mrs. Keylon had so enthralled their youngsters, often putting them in front of the church for special programs and presentations, that their families found themselves with no choice but to come. Their first visit might have been to watch their kids, but the next one was often because the teacher had welcomed them with that same warm and happy voice. Her spirit immediately indicated that she cared, and feeling loved is the best reason anyone has for wanting to come back to any place. This church grew as kids brought their parents, not the other way around.

As one hot, muggy Tennessee summer passed into another, Woody grew from a precocious young boy into a sometimes confident teenager. Not surprisingly, since he was attending a church that loved music, his affection for music grew too. Besides singing in church, he began to perform anywhere people would let him. And maybe because of Mrs. Keylon's influence, he grew keenly aware of each song's message.

Like most teenagers, Woody kept most of his big dreams to himself. Even so, Mrs. Keylon somehow sensed that the boy wanted to pursue music as a career. Unlike so many others, she didn't tell him that it was a dream that few ever achieved. She encouraged him, pushed him forward, let him know she believed in him and that if he wanted it badly enough, he could do it. There can be little doubt that her faith in him was one of the reasons he gave it a try.

Thirty years came and went, and while Woody Wright traveled more miles than he could count, Mrs. Keylon continued to walk down the same road to the same church, sharing the same fascinating Bible stories with new groups of little kids who had also come to know and love her as if she were one of them. As the doors of opportunity closed again and again in Woody's face, age couldn't stop the woman from continuing to open the doors to the gospel for a host of new students. As the musician came close to making his mark time and time again, only to discover the crushing weight of disappointment, Mrs. Keylon told a new generation that as long as they had faith, they could work through all their disappointments. And as Woody stared day after day, month after month, year after year at long highways leading to an even longer string of one-night stands, Mrs. Keylon gazed into the waters of the stream that ran not only by her house and church but through her heart.

"Boy, the attitude she had." Woody spoke with a combination of respect and honor as he remembered. "No matter what happened she was always positive. She always had a good word for anybody in any situation. No matter her age she was young and alive, always looking forward to the next day. Nothing could stop her."

Many things fuel an entertainer's desire to fight the long odds that have been stacked against achieving success. A part of them is the dream of seeing his name in lights, or maybe of hearing his voice on the radio. It might be dreams of money, cars, and large homes. But nothing is as important as his belief in tomorrow. As long as he can go to sleep believing that the next day offers new hope and another chance, he can push on. For Woody, this became as natural as breathing. To understand the source of this attitude, one need only look back to his experience with Mrs. Keylon.

"I was active in the music department of our church," he recalled. "When I sang I felt so alive! I had my own little group of singers I put together with some other high school kids. I got the feeling that when Mrs. Keylon listened to me sing, she thought what I was doing was special. She made me think that I was good, that I had something to offer."

Simply put, Billye Keylon believed that everyone had something to offer. In her mind everyone had a special gift. She believed this so strongly that she never looked back to "the good old days" or thought that the best was in the past. She never resigned herself to acting her age. She felt that each generation brought a vitality that could and would change the world for the better. By working with the youngsters at church, she not only reinforced these beliefs in her own mind but also instilled the seeds of her belief in the minds and hearts of all the children who grew to love her.

Woody Wright left the church and Kingston and headed for Music City. He finally got his first career break in 1992, becoming a part of the trio Matthews, Wright, and King. Though the trio earned a reputation as being one of the most talented groups in country music, the group failed to make a dent in the crowded country music field. Other doors opened but seemed to close just as quickly. About the only thing that kept Woody going was his faith that someone somewhere would recognize his talent like his old Sunday school teacher had so many years before.

At the end of the nineties Woody was introduced to Bill Gaither, who was looking for new material for his Homecoming concert. Wright dove into this challenge with the same enthusiasm he had once seen in Mrs. Keylon's Sunday school class. After trying to make it in country music, Wright now realized the door Mrs. Keylon had once opened for him was now reopened, asking him to come home.

Woody Wright has now written dozens of new Christian songs, arranged performances for the famous Gaither Homecoming series, and performs in churches on a regular basis. He has found success in the same kind of music and message he knew as a child.

During occasional breaks, Woody Wright takes solitary walks along the road between Heavenly Hollow and Bugger Bottom. There in the shade of the centuries-old trees, he stares into the water and thinks of a woman whose earthly walks have ended. As a summer breeze rustles the leaves, he can almost hear her girlish giggle and feel her hand on his shoulder. But even more than those once tangible elements of their relationship, he can easily sense her spirit all around him and still see the love in her eyes.

The legend about the stream may be true. The Lord very well may have dipped His hand into the water and given it special properties that would bring peace, health, and comfort. Still, there was no way that Woody or anyone else could really prove it.

But beyond a shadow of a doubt, Woody knew that the Lord had reached down His hand and left His imprint on Billye Keylon's heart. Woody saw it and felt it time and time again. He saw the Lord through everything she did. He felt his faith through her faith in him.

"She'd love what I'm doing now." He smiled. "You know," he added, "all those people in that church really influenced me. That whole deal I experienced there brought me up right. But she was the one who got me excited and kept me coming back."

Coming back not only anchored his life but gave Woody a mission. His excitement, his energy, and his message are the same as Billye Keylon's. Through his incredible music, he knows that his Sunday school teacher's faith is now touching a new generation.

Stories Behind the Best-Loved Songs of Christmas

Ace Collins

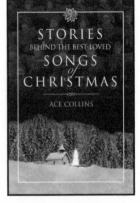

Taking you inside the nativity of over thirty favorite songs and carols, Ace Collins introduces you to people you've never met, stories you've never heard, and meanings you'd never have imagined.

From the rollicking appeal of "Jingle Bells" to the tranquil beauty of "Silent Night," the great songs of Christmas contain messages of peace, hope, and truth, and celebrates the birth of God's greatest gift to the world—Jesus, the most wonderful Christmas song of all.

Jacketed Hardcover: 0310239265

Also available:
The Stories Behind the Great Traditions of Christmas is full of the fascinating stories behind traditions such as the Yule log, stockings, mistletoe, holly, and more.
Jacketed Hardcover: 0310248809

Available October 2006:
More Stories Behind the Best-Loved Songs of Christmas. Hear these familiar melodies with new understanding as their stories find their way into your heart.
Jacketed Hardcover: 031026314X

Stories Behind the Hymns That Inspire America

Ace Collins

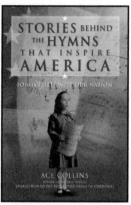

From the moment the pilgrims landed on the shores of the New World, to the dark days following September 11th, songs of faith have inspired, comforted, and rallied our beloved country. The stories behind these songs will fascinate you and bring new meaning and richness to special spiritual moments in the history of our nation. Discover how:

- "Faith of Our Fathers," sung at Franklin Delano Roosevelt's funeral, had its roots not with the pilgrims but with a Catholic fighting for the right to worship freely in Anglican England.
- World events, from the downing of Flight 007 in Russian airspace to Desert Storm and September 11th, propelled Lee Greenwood's "God Bless the U.S.A."
- Combining African rhythms and Southern folk melodies, slaves brought Bible truths to life with songs such as "Roll, Jordan, Roll."

Jacketed Hardcover: 0310248795

We want to hear from you. Please send your comments about this book to us in care of zreview@zondervan.com. Thank you.

GRAND RAPIDS, MICHIGAN 49530 USA

WWW.ZONDERVAN.COM

ZONDERVAN.COM/
AUTHORTRACKER